Wolfgang Amadè Mozart

Wolfgang Amadeus
Mozart

Johannes Jansen

TASCHEN

KÖLN LONDON MADRID NEW YORK PARIS TOKYO

Cover:
Wolfgang Amadeus Mozart
Painting by Barbara Krafft, 1819

Back cover:
Mozart, aged 14
Painting by Saverio Dalla Rosa, 1770

Front flap and illustration page 2:
Mozart at the piano
Unfinished painting by Joseph Lange, 1789

Inner front flap:
"Family Portrait"
Anonymous, c. 1780/81

Back flap:
The "Champagne Aria" (*Don Giovanni*); Francisco d'Andrade on stage
Painting by Max Slevogt, 1902

Inner back flap:
***Requiem*. Mozart's autograph notebook, 1790**

Page 2:
The 6-year-old Mozart in court dress
Painting by Pietro Antonio Lorenzoni (attributed), 1763

© 1999 Benedikt Taschen Verlag GmbH
Hohenzollernring 53, D–50672 Köln

Edited by Michael Konze, Cologne
English translation: Sally Schreiber, Cologne
French translation: Catherine Henry, Nancy,
and Michèle Schreyer, Cologne
Cover design: Catinka Keul, Cologne

Printed in Spain
ISBN 3–8228–6614–8

Inhalt | Contents | Sommaire

Kindheit in Salzburg

A Childhood in Salzburg

Salzburg um die Mitte des 18. Jahrhunderts ist die Hauptstadt eines politisch selbständigen Erzbistums zwischen Österreich und Bayern. Das musikalische Zentrum ist der fürsterzbischöfliche Hof. Hier versieht Leopold Mozart das Amt eines zweiten Violinisten. Nach Salzburg gekommen war der Augsburger Buchbinderssohn als Student der Philosophie und Rechte, doch seine eigentliche Berufung lag in der Musik. Im zweiten Studienjahr wegen zu häufigen Fernbleibens der Universität verwiesen, fand er zunächst eine Anstellung als Musiker und Kammerdiener beim Domherren Graf Thurn-Valsassina. 1747, vier Jahre nach seinem Eintritt in die erzbischöfliche Hofkapelle, heiratet er die Salzburger Beamtentochter Anna Maria Pertl. Von ihren sieben Kindern überleben nur zwei, das erste, Maria Anna Walburga, wird 1751 geboren, das zweite, ein Sohn, fünf Jahre später; die lateinische Taufurkunde vom 28. Januar 1756, ausgestellt am Tag nach der Geburt, lautet auf die Namen Johannes Chrysostomus Wolfgangus Theophilus.

Wolfgang Amadé, wie er sich später selbst nennen wird, hat einen recht berühmten Vater. Leopold Mozarts im Geburtsjahr des Sohnes veröffentlichter „Versuch einer Gründlichen Violinschule" macht ihn als Geiger, Lehrer und Komponisten weit über die Landesgrenzen hinaus bekannt. Doch sein beruflicher Aufstieg in der Hofkapelle – 1757 erhält er den Titel eines Hof- und Kammerkomponisten, 1763 wird er zum Vize-Kapellmeister ernannt – verläuft weniger steil als erhofft, und ein Grund dafür sind zweifellos die Kinder, deren Erziehung ihm zur Lebensaufgabe wird. Beider musikalisches Talent macht sich früh bemerkbar, besonders frappant beim jüngsten: „Er unterhielte sich oft lange zeit bey dem Clavier mit zusammen suchen der Terzen, welche er immer anstimmte, und sein Wohlgefallen verrieth daß es wohl klang", erinnert sich die ältere Schwester. Hingebungsvoll treibt Leopold die Ausbildung von ‚Nannerl' und ‚Wolfgangerl' nicht nur auf musikalischem Gebiet voran. Unermüdlich hält er sie zum Lernen an, schreibt Übungsstücke und stellt Notenbücher zusammen, die auch heute noch Bestandteil jedes Klavierunterrichts sind.

Wie vor ihm die Schwester durcheilt Mozart alle Stationen auf dem Weg zum perfekten Pianisten, aber er

In the middle of the 18th century, Salzburg was the capital of a politically independent archbishopric situated between Austria and Bavaria. The court of the prince-archbishop was not only the governmental but also the musical center of the land, and here Leopold Mozart served as second violinist in the court orchestra. Born the son of a bookbinder in Augsburg, Leopold had originally come to Salzburg to study philosophy and law. But his true vocation was music. After expulsion from the university in his second year for poor attendance, he initially took up a position as court and chamber musician to the cathedral canon, Count Thurn-Valsassina. In 1747, after four years in the archbishop's *Hofkapelle*, Leopold married Anna Maria Pertl, daughter of a Salzburg civil servant. Of their seven children, only two survived: Maria Anna Walburga, born in 1751, and a son born five years later. The baptismal certificate of January 28, 1756, the day after the birth, records the name of the child as Johannes Chrysostomus Wolfgangus Theophilus.

Wolfgang Amadé, as he would later call himself, was the son of a quite famous father. A musical tract, *Versuch einer Gründlichen Violinschule*, published in the same year his son was born, had carried the name of Leopold Mozart as violinist, teacher and composer far beyond the borders of the archbishopric. He rose to the position of official court and chamber composer the following year, and to vice-*Kapellmeister* in 1763. Nevertheless, Leopold's career progressed more slowly than he hoped—doubles in part because of his devotion to raising his children, both of whom displayed musical talent at an early age. The boy in particular seemed to possess amazing gifts. In later years his sister recalled, "He often entertained himself at length at the piano seeking out thirds, which he always found by ear, and he showed his delight at the harmony." Leopold passionately fostered the education of "Nannerl" and "Wolfgangerl" in all areas; in music he held them indefatigably to their tasks, writing practice pieces for them and compiling music books that remain a part of all piano instruction to this day.

Together with his sister, the young Mozart quickly progressed along the road to becoming an excellent

Une enfance salzbourgeoise

Vers le milieu du 18ᵉ siècle, Salzbourg est la capitale
d'un archevêché politiquement autonome situé entre
l'Autriche et la Bavière, et dont le centre musical est la
cour des princes-archevêques. C'est là que Léopold
Mozart occupe un poste de deuxième violon. Ce fils d'un
relieur d'Augsbourg était venu à Salzbourg pour y faire
des études de philosophie et de droit, mais c'est la
musique qui était sa véritable vocation. Renvoyé de
l'université au bout de deux ans pour des absences trop
souvent répétées, il trouva d'abord une place de musicien et de valet de chambre chez le comte et chanoine de
Thurn-Valsassina. En 1747, quatre ans après son entrée
à la chapelle princière, il épouse Anna Maria Pertl, la
fille d'un fonctionnaire de Salzbourg. Sur leurs sept
enfants, deux seulement survivront, le premier, Maria
Anna Walburga, née en 1751, et le second, un fils né
cinq ans plus tard. L'extrait de baptême, rédigé en latin,
est délivré le lendemain de la naissance aux noms de
Johannes Chrysostomus Wolfgangus Theophilus.
   Wolfgang Amadé, ainsi qu'il s'appellera lui-même
par la suite, a un père très renommé. La publication,
l'année de la naissance de son fils, de son «Essai de
méthode approfondie de violon», le fait connaître bien
au-delà des frontières du pays en tant que violoniste,
professeur et compositeur. Son avancement profes-
sionnel au sein de la chapelle princière – il obtient en
1757 le titre de compositeur de la cour et de la chambre
princières et il est nommé en 1763 vice-maître de
chapelle – est cependant moins fulgurant qu'escompté.
Une des raisons en est sans doute les enfants et leur
éducation, à laquelle il se consacre entièrement. Ils ont
tous deux une disposition pour la musique qui se fait
très tôt sentir, en particulier chez le plus jeune. «Il
s'amusait souvent pendant des heures à chercher des
tierces au piano ; il les chantonnait toujours, et on savait
à voir son plaisir que ça sonnait bien», se souvient la
sœur aînée. Léopold continue avec ferveur d'assurer la
formation de «Nannerl» et de «Wolfgangerl», sans se
limiter au seul domaine musical. Il les exhorte inlas-
sablement à l'étude, écrit des exercices et compose des
recueils de musique qui, aujourd'hui encore, figurent
dans tout bon enseignement du piano.

Das Mozart-Porträt von Barbara Krafft
entstand postum im Jahre 1819.
Seite 8 und 9: Der Vater Leopold Mozart
(1719–1786) zur Zeit der Veröffent-
lichung seiner „Violinschule" (1756).
Die P. A. Lorenzini zugeschriebenen
Porträts der Mutter und der Schwester
entstanden 1770 bzw. 1773.

The portrait of Mozart by Barbara Krafft
was painted posthumously (1819).
Pages 8 and 9: Mozart's father, Leopold
(1719–1786), at the time of the publication of his tract *Violinschule* (1756). The
portraits of Mozart's mother and his
sister, painted in 1770 and 1773 respect-
ively, are attributed to P. A. Lorenzoni.

Barbara Krafft réalisa ce portrait de
Mozart après la mort de celui-ci, en 1819.
Pages 8 et 9 : Le père de Mozart, Léopold
(1719–1786) à l'époque où parut son
«Ecole du violon» (1756). Portraits de la
mère de Mozart et de sa sœur, attribués à
P. A. Lorenzoni et peints en 1770 et 1773.

Sinfonia

Uno.

Divert:

Fuga

Leop: Mozart

G. Eichler delin.

Iac. Andr. Fridrich Se. A.V.

CONVENIT IGITUR---IN GESTU NEC
VENUSTATEM CONSPICUAM, NEC TURPITU
=DINEM ESSE, NE AUT HISTRIONES,
AUT OPERARII VIDEAMUR ESSE. Cic. Rhet. ad Her. Lib. 3. XV.

spielt auch Geige, und mit kaum fünf Jahren komponiert er erste kleine Werke wie das Andante und Allegro für Klavier (KV 1a/b) – eine Tatsache, die mit Drill allein nicht zu erklären ist. Ganz offensichtlich bricht sich hier eine Begabung Bahn, die auch den ehrgeizigen Vater in Erstaunen versetzt und ihn alsbald kühne Reisepläne schmieden läßt. Denn um dieses Wunder der musikalischen Welt zu präsentieren, ist Salzburg nicht der rechte Ort.

Am 12. Januar 1762 macht sich Leopold mit den Kindern nach München auf, wo sie am Hof des bayrischen Kurfürsten musizieren. Im September steht die zweite Reise an, diesmal mitsamt der Mutter und in Begleitung eines Dieners. Über Passau geht es nach Linz, wo Wolfgang sein erstes öffentliches Konzert absolviert. In Windeseile verbreitet sich die Kunde von den Wunderkindern bis nach Wien – das eigentliche Ziel der Reise. Nach einer Zwischenstation in Ybbs treffen die Mozarts am 6. Oktober ein, und schon eine Woche später gewähren ihnen Kaiser und Kaiserin Audienz in Schloß Schön-

pianist. In addition, the boy also studied the violin, and at barely five years of age already had composed short works for that instrument, as well as a first Andante and Allegro for the piano (K 1a/b)—an achievement that cannot be accounted for by drill work alone. The boy clearly demonstrated a level of talent that astounded even the ambitious father, who responded by immediately forging bold plans for travel: Salzburg was not the right stage on which to present the musical world with such a musical miracle.

On January 12, 1762, Leopold set out with the children for Munich, where the Wolfgang and Nannerl performed at the court of the Bavarian Elector. In September, now accompanied by the mother and a servant, they undertook a second tour, this time to Passau and Linz, where Wolfgang gave his first public concert. With the speed of lightning, news of the child prodigies traveled to Vienna, capital of the Austro-Hungarian empire, and the true goal of the family's journey. After a stopover in Ybbs, the family arrived in Vienna on October 6, and

Das Geburtshaus in der Salzburger Getreidegasse. Anonymes Gemälde vom Anfang des 19. Jahrhunderts. Seit 1773 wohnt die Familie Mozart am Makartplatz (vormals Hannibalplatz). Die Wohnung verfügt über sieben Zimmer und einen geräumigen Saal, der zum Musizieren genutzt wird und auch Platz für Klaviere bietet, die Leopold Mozart in Kommission verkauft. Das unten abgebildete Photo entstand um 1900.

The house where Mozart was born in the Salzburger Getreidegasse. Anonymous painting from the early 19th century. After 1773, the family occupied a house on the market square (Marktplatz, formerly Hannibalsplatz) in Salzburg. The apartment had more than seven rooms and a spacious hall where the family played music together and which was even large enough for the pianos that Leopold Mozart sold on commission. The bottom photograph was taken in 1900.

La maison natale de Mozart dans la Getreidegasse à Salzbourg. Peinture anonyme du début du 19ᵉ siècle. La famille Mozart habite sur la Makartplatz (anciennement Hannibalplatz) de Salzbourg à partir de 1773. Le logement comprend sept pièces et une salle de belles proportions où l'on fait de la musique et où sont entreposés les pianos que Léopold Mozart vend en commission. La photographie ci-dessous a été prise vers 1900.

Comme sa sœur avant lui, Mozart brûle toutes les étapes du chemin qui doit faire de lui un parfait pianiste, mais il joue aussi du violon et à peine âgé de cinq ans, il compose déjà de petites œuvres comme l'andante et l'allegro pour piano (K. 1a/b), ce que le «dressage» ne saurait à lui seul expliquer. Il est tout à fait évident que nous sommes là en présence de l'émergence d'un don dont ce père ambitieux est lui-même ébahi, lequel va dès lors s'empresser de faire d'audacieux projets de voyage. Car pour présenter ce prodige au monde musical, Salzbourg n'est pas le bon endroit.

Le 12 janvier 1762, Léopold part avec ses enfants pour Munich, où ils se produisent à la cour du prince électeur de Bavière. En septembre a lieu le second voyage, auquel se joint cette fois la mère, accompagnée d'un domestique. Après Passau, on les trouve à Linz où Wolfgang donne son premier concert en public. La nouvelle des enfants prodiges se répand comme une traînée de poudre jusqu'à Vienne, but effectif du voyage. Après une escale à Ybbs, les Mozart y parviennent le 6 octobre et dès la semaine suivante, l'empereur et l'impératrice leur accordent une audience au château de Schönbrunn. Marie-Thérèse offre aux enfants des tenues de gala et fait remettre à la famille 100 ducats, assortis du désir qu'elle veuille bien séjourner encore quelque temps à Vienne.

Das ‚fammiliengemälde' entstand 1780/81, zwei Jahre nach dem Tod der Mutter. Der Maler des Bildes ist unbekannt, jedenfalls ist es neueren Forschungen zufolge nicht der vielfach genannte Johann Nepomuk Della Croce.

The "family portrait" was painted in 1780/81, two years after the death of Mozart's mother. The painter is unknown; recent research has in any case disproved the widely circulated belief that the artist was Johann Nepomuk Della Croce.

Le « portrait de famille » a été réalisé en 1780/81, deux ans après la mort de la mère de Mozart. On ignore qui l'a peint, en tout cas les recherches récentes ont révélé qu'il ne s'agit pas de Johann Nepomuk Della Croce, souvent nommé.

brunn. Maria Theresia schenkt den Kindern Galakleider und läßt 100 Dukaten überreichen, verbunden mit dem Wunsch, daß die Familie noch eine Weile in Wien bleiben möge. Aber auch der ungarische Adel ist neugierig auf die Sensation, also führt ein Abstecher nach Preßburg, ehe man sich Ende Dezember, reich beschenkt, wieder aus Wien verabschiedet.

Das neue Jahr beginnt nicht sorgenlos, denn Wolfgang kränkelt zum wiederholten Mal. Attacken von Gelenkrheumatismus und andere Krankheiten überschatten seine Kindheit. Daß sie ursächlich mit den Reisestrapazen zusammenhängen, ist nicht auszuschließen, aber sicher wäre es falsch, Leopold Mozart dafür verantwortlich zu machen oder gar zu unterstellen, er habe die Gesundheit seines Kindes bewußt aufs Spiel gesetzt. Denn daß er ein umsichtiger und fürsorglicher Vater war, ist nicht zu bestreiten.

Im Februar 1763, gerade sieben Jahre alt, tritt Wolfgang zusammen mit seiner Schwester erstmals am Hof des Salzburger Fürsterzbischofs Graf Schrattenbach auf. Er ist der Familie Mozart wohlgesonnen, was sich vor allem darin zeigt, daß er großzügig Urlaub für Leopold Mozarts Reiseunternehmungen gewährt. Am 9. Juni 1763 setzt sich der Familientroß erneut in Bewegung. Ziel der Reise, die mehr als drei Jahre dauern wird, sind London und Paris, die beiden großen Musikzentren Westeuropas.

one week later, the Emperor and Empress granted them an audience in their palace at Schönbrunn. Maria Theresia presented the children with court clothing and 100 ducats along with the wish that the family remain in Vienna for some time. The Hungarian nobility, too, was curious about the new sensation. The family therefore travelled to Pressburg (today Bratislava) before finally leaving Vienna once again at the end of December and returning home, showered with gifts.

The new year did not begin smoothly, however, for Wolfgang fell sick repeatedly—his childhood was in fact plagued by joint rheumatism and other ailments. Although the rigors of the tours may have had something to do with his susceptibility, it would be false to hold Leopold Mozart responsible for the weakness, or even to accuse him of consciously taking risks with his child's health. There can be no question that he was a prudent and solicitous father.

In February 1763, Wolfgang, age seven, and his sister gave their first performance at the court of the prince-bishop of Salzburg, Count Schrattenbach. The nobleman looked with favor on the Mozarts, granting Leopold a leave of absence in order to undertake further tours. On June 9, 1763, the family train set out once more. This time, in a journey that was to last more than three years, they set their sights on London and Paris, the two biggest musical centers of Western Europe.

Reverendiſſimus
et Eelſiſſimus
Dominus Dominus
SIGISMUNDUS CHRISTOPHORUS
Archiepiscopus et S. R. I. Princeps
Salisburgensis, Sacræ Sedis Apostolicæ
Legatus Natus, Germaniæ Primas,
ex Illustma Prosapiā Comitum
de Schrattenbach
&c. &c.

Mais la noblesse hongroise est elle aussi curieuse de découvrir cette sensation ; aussi fait-on un crochet par Presbourg [ancien nom de Bratislava, alors capitale de la Hongrie habsbourgeoise, N.d.T.] avant de prendre à nouveau congé de Vienne, comblé de présents, à la fin décembre.

Le début de la nouvelle année n'est pas sans apporter des soucis, car Wolfgang ne cesse de tomber malade. Son enfance est assombrie par des rhumatismes articulaires et autres maladies. Il n'est pas à exclure qu'elles aient leur origine dans la fatigue engendrée par les voyages, mais il serait certainement erroné d'en rendre responsable Léopold Mozart ou même de laisser entendre qu'il aurait délibérément mis en péril la santé de son enfant. On ne saurait en effet contester qu'il ait été un père prudent et attentionné. En février 1763, Wolfgang, tout juste âgé de sept ans, fait pour la première fois son entrée, avec sa sœur, à la cour du prince-archevêque de Salzbourg, le comte de Schrattenbach. La bienveillance de celui-ci envers la famille Mozart se manifeste surtout à travers le fait qu'il accorde généreusement un congé à Léopold Mozart pour lui permettre d'entreprendre ses voyages. Le 9 juin 1763, la petite famille se remet en route, avec pour objectifs de ce nouveau voyage, qui durera plus de trois ans, Londres et Paris, les deux grands centres musicaux de l'Europe occidentale.

Thronfolger Joseph II. stellt Mozart der Kaiserin Maria Theresia vor. Das Wohlwollen des nachmaligen Kaisers bleibt Mozart auch in seinen späteren Wiener Jahren erhalten. Gemälde von Eduard Ender, 1869

Seite 12: Leopold Mozarts Dienstherr Sigismund Christoph Graf von Schrattenbach (1698–1771), von 1753 bis 1771 regierender Fürsterzbischof in Salzburg. Kolorierter Kupferstich von Joseph Sebastian und Johann Baptist Klauber, um 1760

Salzburg, die barocke Residenz am Fuß der Alpen, ist eine Stadt mit südlichem Flair, geprägt von der Baulust geistlicher Potentaten. Kolorierter Kupferstich von Johann Friedrich Probst, um 1750

Joseph II, successor to the Austrian throne, presents Mozart to Empress Maria Theresia. Mozart retained the favor of the future emperor even in his later years in Vienna. Painting by Eduard Ender, 1869

Page 12: Leopold Mozart's overlord, Sigismund Christoph, Count von Schrattenbach (1698–1771) presided as prince-archbishop from 1753 to 1771. Colored copperplate engraving by Joseph Sebastian and Johann Baptist Klauber, c. 1760

Salzburg, the baroque *Residenz* lying at the foot of the Alps is a city with a southern flair, marked by the enthusiasm for building shown by its spiritual potentates. Colored copperplate by Johann Friedrich Probst, c. 1750

Le prince héritier Joseph II présente Mozart à l'impératrice Marie-Thérèse. Au cours des années à Vienne qui suivront, la faveur de l'empereur lui restera acquise. Tableau d'Eduard Ender, 1869

Page 12 : Le maître de Léopold Mozart, Sigismund Christoph comte de Schrattenbach (1698–1771), de 1753 à 1771 prince-archevêque de Salzbourg. Eau-forte coloriée de Joseph Sebastian et Johann Baptist Klauber, vers 1760

Salzbourg, résidence baroque au pied des Alpes, a la grâce des villes du midi et elle est marquée par le désir de construire des princes de l'Eglise. Eau-forte coloriée de Johann Friedrich Probst, vers 1750

Auf der Spur des Erfolgs

On the Trail of Success

Die große Reise des Jahres 1763 beginnt mit einer Panne. Ein Radbruch am eigens angeschafften Reisewagen zwingt die Familie zu einem zweitägigen Zwischenstopp in Wasserburg am Inn. Leopold nutzt die Wartezeit, um seinem Sohn an der Orgel der Stadtkirche das Pedalspiel zu erklären. Obwohl er mit seinen Beinen die Pedale kaum erreicht, kommt er auf Anhieb – im Stehen – damit zurecht. Wundersame Begebenheiten wie diese lassen das Kind wie ein Wesen von einem anderen Stern erscheinen. Nannerl, so verblüffend auch ihre Talente sind, verblaßt daneben mehr und mehr. Die Zukunftshoffnungen der Familie ruhen ganz allein auf Wolfgang, und um sie wahrzumachen, vernachlässigt Leopold die eigene Karriere, verschuldet sich, ja er riskiert sogar den Hinauswurf aus der Hofkapelle, indem er den ihm gewährten Urlaub mehrfach überzieht.

Nach München und Augsburg, wo man ein leicht zu transportierendes Clavichord (›Reiseklavier‹) erwirbt, das vor allem zum Üben dient, macht die Familie Halt in Ulm, Stuttgart, Mannheim und in verschiedenen anderen Städten und Residenzen, ehe sie über Köln und Aachen die Grenze zu den damals österreichischen Niederlanden erreicht. Bis zur Ankunft in Brüssel am 4. Oktober 1763 haben die Kinder schon rund zwanzig, teils öffentliche, teils private Auftritte absolviert und dabei nicht wenig Geld eingespielt. Nannerl erinnert sich in späteren Jahren, daß sie sich dort, wo kein Konzert zustande kam, jeweils nur so lange aufhielten, „bis sie alle Merkwürdigkeiten gesehen hatten". Auch wenn der touristische Aspekt für ihn sicher nicht vorrangig ist, enthält der Vater seinen Kindern, schon aus eigenem Bildungsinteresse, keine Sehenswürdigkeit vor; in Heidelberg z.B. wird neben dem Schloß und dem damals als Weltwunder bestaunten „Großen Faß" (das größte Weinfaß der Welt, mit einem Fassungsvermögen von über 2210 Hektolitern) auch eine Tapeten- und Seidenwirkerei besichtigt.

Neben dem finanziellen Ertrag kann Leopold vor allem zahlreiche Kontakte mit Musikern und Angehörigen des Adels als Gewinn verbuchen. Ausgestattet mit ihren Empfehlungsschreiben, öffnen sich ihm auch die Türen der Adelshäuser in Paris. Dort rührt Baron Fried-

The great tour of 1763 began with an accident. A broken wheel on the carriage they had purchased for themselves forced the family into a two-day layover in Wasserburg on the Inn. Leopold took advantage of the delay, however, to explain to his son the use of the pedals on the organ of the city church. Although the boy's legs were hardly long enough to reach, by standing on the pedals, Wolfgang succeeded in his very first attempt at playing. The boy's wondrous abilities seemed to place him in another dimension; Nannerl, in spite of her own amazing gifts, paled more and more by comparison. The family's hopes for the future thus came to rest on Wolfgang alone, and to fulfill these dreams, Leopold not only neglected his own career and went into debt, but even risked being thrown out of the court orchestra by drastically prolonging his permitted leave.

After Munich and Augsburg, where the family obtained a portable piano intended primarily for practice, they visited Ulm, Stuttgart, Mannheim and various other cities and courts, before reaching Cologne, and Aachen and finally the border of the Austrian Netherlands. By their arrival in Brussels on October 4, 1763, the children had already performed approximately twenty times, sometimes publicly, sometimes privately, and had thus brought in no little sum of money. In later years Nannerl recalled that in the places where no concert could be arranged, the family stayed only "until they had seen all the sights." Even though the tourist aspect of the journey was certainly not the primary one, Leopold, for the sake of his children's education, saw to it that they missed nothing that might be of interest. In Heidelberg, for example, in addition to touring the palace and viewing the "Great Barrel"—the largest vine vessel in the world which, with a capacity of more than 2,210 hectoliters (approximately 49,000 gallons), was admired at the time a world wonder—they also visited a carpet and silk manufactory. Besides the financial gain, Leopold was also able to tally up numerous contacts with musicians and members of the nobility. Fitted out with their letters of recommendation, he gained entry even to the houses of the Parisian nobility. Baron Friedrich Melchior von Grimm, secretary to the duke of Orléans

Sur la voie du succès

Le grand voyage de 1763 commence par une panne. La rupture d'une roue de la voiture qu'elle a spécialement achetée pour ce voyage contraint la famille à faire une halte de deux jours à Wasserburg sur l'Inn. Léopold met à profit cette attente pour expliquer à son fils le fonctionnement du pédalier sur l'orgue de l'église de la ville. Bien que ses jambes touchent à peine les pédales, celui-ci s'en tire du premier coup... mais debout ! Des faits aussi surprenants que celui-ci donnent de l'enfant l'image d'un être venu d'une autre planète. Aussi stupéfiants que puissent être ses propres dons, Nannerl à côté de lui fait figure de plus en plus pâle. Les espérances d'avenir de la famille reposent uniquement sur Wolfgang, et pour les faire devenir réalité, Léopold néglige sa propre carrière, s'endette et frôle même le renvoi de la chapelle princière pour avoir à plusieurs reprises outrepassé la durée du congé qui lui était alloué.

Après Munich et Augsbourg, où on acquiert un clavicorde facilement transportable qui sert surtout à s'exercer, la famille fait étape à Ulm, Stuttgart, Mannheim ainsi que dans plusieurs autres villes et résidences, avant de traverser Cologne et Aix-la-Chapelle pour atteindre la frontière de ce qui était alors les Pays-Bas autrichiens. Jusqu'à leur arrivée à Bruxelles le 4 octobre 1763, les enfants ont fait une vingtaine d'apparitions, tantôt publiques, tantôt privées, – source de rentrées d'argent non négligeables. Des années plus tard, Nannerl se souvient que, dans les endroits où il n'y avait pas de concert, ils restaient toujours «jusqu'à ce qu'ils aient vu tout ce qu'il y avait à voir». Même si l'aspect touristique n'est certainement pas pour lui d'une importance primordiale, le père ne prive jamais ses enfants, ne serait-ce que par son intérêt personnel pour la culture, de l'occasion de voir une curiosité. C'est ainsi par exemple qu'à Heidelberg, à côté du château et du «gros tonneau» devant lequel on s'extasiait alors comme devant une des merveilles du monde (le plus gros tonneau à vin du monde, d'une capacité de 2210 hectolitres environ), ils visitèrent également un atelier de fabrication de tentures et un autre de tissage de la soie.

Outre le gain financier, Léopold a surtout à son actif de nouer de nombreux contacts avec des musiciens

Landkarte des Bistums Salzburg im 18. Jahrhundert. Kolorierter Kupferstich von Johann Baptist Homann, gedruckt 1745

Map of the archbishopric of Salzburg, 18th century. Colored copperplate engraving by Johann Baptist Homann, printed 1745

Carte de l'évêché de Salzbourg au 18e siècle. Eau-forte coloriée de Johann Baptist Homann, imprimée en 1745

rich Melchior von Grimm, Sekretär des Herzogs von Orléans und Herausgeber der ›Correspondance littéraire‹, publizistisch die Trommel für die Mozart-Kinder, und der Erfolg läßt nicht lange auf sich warten. Schon in den Weihnachtstagen des Jahres 1763, kaum vier Wochen nach ihrem Eintreffen in Paris, erhält die Familie Audienz bei Ludwig XV. und Madame Pompadour in Versailles.

Die Aura des Wunderkindes, das sein Publikum mit Kunststücken auf der Geige und „Phantasiren" am Klavier entzückt, erhält eine neue Dimension, als Leopold in Paris die ersten Kompositionen seines Sohnes stechen läßt: „Stellen Sie sich den lermen für, den diese Sonaten in der Welt machen werden, wann am Titlblat stehet daß es ein Werk eines Kindes von 7 Jahren ist", schreibt er nach Salzburg; gehörigen Eindruck soll auch die Widmung machen, denn sie gilt keiner Geringeren als der Königstochter Louise-Marie-Thérèse de Bourbon. Tatsächlich handelt es sich bei diesem „Opus 1" mit zwei Sonaten für Klavier und Violine (KV 6 und 7) – parallel erscheint auch ein Sonatenpaar „Opus 2" (KV 8 und 9) – um eine Zusammenstellung von Salzburger Klavierstücken, die Mozart seinem Vater ins Notenbuch ›diktiert‹ hatte, ehe er noch selbst Noten schreiben konnte. Daß Leopold bei der Ausarbeitung und Reinschrift in Paris mit Hand anlegte, gilt als sicher, doch im Kern sind es eigenständige Kompositionen, nur bereichert um einige diskrete Anleihen bei Komponisten aus dem Pariser Bekanntenkreis.

Beflügelt von den Erfolgen in Paris, nimmt Leopold das nächste große Ziel in Angriff: London. Am 22. April 1764 schifft sich die Familie in Calais ein und setzt nach England über. Fünf Tage später musizieren die Kinder erstmals vor dem englischen Königspaar in Buckingham-House.

Der Londoner Aufenthalt ist das wohl aufregendste Kapitel der Westeuropareise, denn in England ist alles anders als auf dem Kontinent: Die Gesellschaft ist offener, Standesunterschiede haben weniger Bedeutung, der Kapitalismus blüht – auch im Musikleben. Die Stadt, in der die Abonnementskonzerte erfunden wurden, ist ein Tummelplatz ausländischer Opernstars und Komponisten, die ihr Publikum nicht nur in Theatern und Privathäusern, sondern auch in den öffentlichen Gärten finden. Gründer einer der erfolgreichsten Abonnement-Konzertreihen ist Johann Christian Bach (1735–1782). Dieser

and publisher of the journal *Correspondance littéraire*, drummed up support for the children, and success was not long in coming: Scarcely four weeks after their arrival in Paris, during the Christmas holidays of 1763, the Mozart family was granted an audience by Louis XV and Madame Pompadour in the palace of Versailles.

The young Mozart charmed the public with his feats on the violin and his improvisations on the piano, but the aura surrounding the child prodigy reached a new dimension when Leopold had the first compositions of his son printed. "Imagine what a commotion these sonatas will make in the world when it stands on the title page that they are the work of a seven-year-old child," he wrote back to Salzburg. The dedication of the works, too, aimed at making a proper impression: They were inscribed to no one less than Louise-Marie-Thérèse de Bourbon, the daughter of the king. This "Opus 1," comprising two sonatas for piano and violin (K 6 and 7), appeared simultaneously with an "Opus 2" (K 8 and 9), consisting of a compilation of piano pieces the boy had composed in Salzburg and dictated to his father to transcribe into the notebook while he was still too young to write notes. One must assume that Leopold applied his hand to the composition and to the fair copy in Paris; but at core, the pieces are independent compositions, enriched only by some unobtrusive borrowings from composers within the Parisian circle.

On the wings of their success in Paris, Leopold now set his sites on London, the second great goal of the journey. On April 22, 1764, the family boarded ship at Calais for England. Five days later, the children performed for the first time before the royal couple at Buckingham House.

The family's sojourn in London probably comprised the most exciting chapter in their tour of western Europe, for England was truly a world away from the Continent. Society was more open, class distinctions carried less weight, and capitalism flourished even within the field of music. The city which had invented the concept of the privately organized subscription concert was indeed a marketplace of foreign opera stars and composers who found their audiences not only in theaters and private houses, but also in public gardens. The founder of one of the most successful subscription concerts was Johann Christian Bach. The youngest son of Johann Sebastian Bach, he composed not only Italian

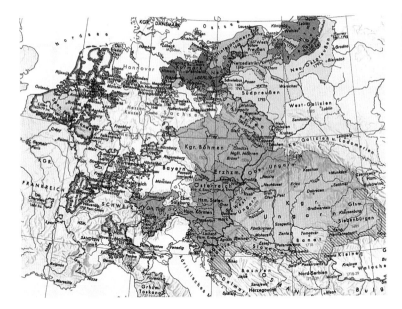

et des membres de la noblesse. Les lettres de recommandation dont il est muni lui ouvrent également les portes des maisons de l'aristocratie parisienne. Le baron Friedrich Melchior von Grimm, secrétaire du duc d'Orléans et éditeur de la «Correspondance littéraire», bat le tambour pour vanter les enfants Mozart, et le succès ne se fait pas longtemps attendre. Dès le jour de Noël de l'an 1763, soit quatre semaines à peine après son arrivée à Paris, la famille obtient une audience de Louis XV et de Madame de Pompadour à Versailles.

L'aura de l'enfant prodige qui transporte son public par des tours de passe-passe au violon et des «improvisations» au piano prend une nouvelle dimension lorsque Léopold fait graver à Paris les premières compositions de son fils. «Imaginez-vous le bruit que feront ces sonates dans le monde quand on verra sur la page de titre que c'est l'œuvre d'un enfant de 7 ans», écrit-il dans une lettre envoyée à Salzbourg. La dédicace doit elle aussi faire son impression, car elle s'adresse à la fille du roi, Louise Marie-Thérèse de Bourbon en personne. Cet «opus 1» de deux sonates pour piano et violon (K. 6 et K. 7) – parallèlement paraît un «opus 2» composé de deux sonates (K. 8 et K. 9) – est en réalité un recueil de pièces pour piano que Mozart avait composées à Salzbourg et qu'il avait «dictées» à son père quand lui-même ne savait pas encore écrire la musique.

Leopold Mozart in selbstbewußter Pose. Porträt, um 1765, P. A. Lorenzoni zugeschrieben
Links: Österreich und Preußen bis 1795
Seite 18: Mozart im Alter von acht Jahren. Gemälde von Johann Zoffany (Zuschreibung), 1764/65. Das nebenstehende Gemälde von Heinrich Lossow (um 1864) zeigt ihn als Knaben an der Orgel der Franziskanerkirche in Ybbs.

Leopold Mozart in a self-assured pose. Portrait, c. 1765, ascribed to P. A. Lorenzoni. Left: Austria and Prussia until 1795
Page 18: Mozart at age eight. The painting is ascribed to Johann Zoffany, 1764/65. The picture next to it, painted by Heinrich Lossow around 1864, depicts the boy Mozart at the organ of the Franciscan church in Ybbs, Austria.

Léopold Mozart, sûr de sa personne. Portrait, vers 1765, attribué à P. A. Lorenzoni
A gauche: L'Autriche et la Prusse avant 1795
Page 18: Mozart à l'âge de huit ans. Tableau attribué à Johann Zoffany, 1764/65. La peinture voisine de Heinrich Lossow (vers 1864) le montre gamin, à l'orgue de l'église des Franciscains de Ybbs.

jüngste Sohn Johann Sebastian Bachs komponiert nicht nur italienische Opern, sondern auch Sinfonien und Klavierkonzerte, deren „singendes Allegro" den jungen Mozart inspiriert.

   In den Sälen von Spring Garden und Renelagh Gardens haben die Mozart-Kinder – vom Vater stets für ein, zwei Jahre jünger ausgegeben, als sie tatsächlich sind –, ihre ersten großen Auftritte. Die Einnahme aus dem ersten beträgt umgerechnet 800 Gulden, was mehr als dem doppelten Jahresgehalt eines Salzburger Hofmusikers entspricht. In Leopold keimen angesichts dieser Verhältnisse nachgerade umstürzlerische Ideen auf: „das hier ist gut, daß das Volk und soviel 1000 ehrlich Leute, die das Brod in dem Schweis ihres Angesichts gewinnen, und die eigentlich den Staat ausmachen und den ganzen Zusammenhang der bürgerlichen Welt erhalten, nicht gezwungen sind wegen etlich 100 ... die ihre Lebenszeit in Überfluss ... zubringen, zu schmachten, und zu leiden." Deutlichere Worte seiner Auflehnung gegen den Absolutismus und das eigene Lakaientum sind nicht überliefert, denn der Brief gerät auf dem Postweg in die Zensur. In der späteren Korrespondenz

opera, but also symphonies and piano concertos whose "singing allegro" inspired the young Mozart. In the halls of Spring Garden and Renelagh Gardens the Mozart children—always promoted by their father as a year or two younger than they actually were—made their first great appearances. The intake from their initial performance alone was approximately 800 gulden, more than twice the annual income of a court musician in Salzburg. The disproportion aroused subversive ideas in Leopold: "It is a good thing here, that the population as a whole and so many 1000s of simple people, who earn their bread by the sweat of their brow and who really make up the state and maintain the whole fabric of the bourgeois world, are not forced to languish and suffer because of some 100 [deleted] who spend their lives in [deleted] overabundance." Any clearer expressions of his opposition to absolutism and his sense of his own position as a lackey have not survived because parts of this letter as well as other writings passed as a matter of course through the hands of the postal censors. Later, father and son would correspond over confidential matters in code.

zwischen Vater und Sohn werden vertrauliche Dinge in Geheimschrift abgefaßt.

Am 13. Mai 1765 treten die beiden Kinder noch einmal öffentlich auf, angeblich mit der C-Dur-Sonate für Klavier zu vier Händen (KV 19d), deren Echtheit allerdings bezweifelt wird. Danach scheint das Interesse an den Wunderkindern abzunehmen. Leopold sieht sich veranlaßt, im „Public Advertiser" zu inserieren, daß, „wer die jungen Wunder privat hören möchte", dies täglich von eins bis drei Uhr nachmittags tun könne. Verlangt er im Mai noch einen Eintritt von fünf Schilling pro Person, sind es im Juli nur noch zwei Schilling und sechs Pence. Ende des Monats besteigt er mit seiner Familie die Fähre nach Calais, läßt den dort geparkten Reisewagen anspannen und nimmt Kurs auf die großen Städte in Flandern und Holland. Das Hauptziel ist Den Haag. Eine Einladung dorthin hatte noch in England der holländische Gesandte Jan Walraad Graf Walderen ausgesprochen.

Holland ist eines der Zentren des Musikverlagswesens in Europa. In Haarlem erscheint 1766 Leopold Mozarts Violinschule auf niederländisch in einer durch die Verwendung des Typen- statt des gebräuchlicheren Plattendrucks bemerkenswerten Edition, zu deren ersten Besitzern der 18jährige Prinz Willem V. von Oranien gehört. Die im Auftrag des Königshauses entstandenen Violinsonaten Opus 4 (KV 26–31) kommen in Den Haag im Druck heraus.

On May 13, 1765, the children once more gave a public performance, supposedly playing the C-Major Sonata for four hands (K 19d), whose validity is however uncertain. Afterwards, interest in the prodigies seemed to wane, and Leopold felt it necessary to announce in the Public Advertiser that anyone "who wished to hear the young wonders privately" might do so between one and three o'clock in the afternoon. Whereas Leopold had been able to command an admission fee of five shillings in May, by July the price had fallen to merely two shillings six pence. At the end of the month, the family returned by ferry to Calais, hitched up their carriage once more, and set off for the large cities in Flanders and Holland.

Their primary goal was The Hague, to which the Dutch envoy, Jan Walraad, Count Walderen, had extended an invitation while the family was still in England.

Holland was one of the musical centers of Europe. Leopold Mozart's Violinschule had been published in 1766 in Haarlem in a type-printing process rather than the usual plate press. One of the very first persons to acquire the book was the eighteen-year-old Prince William V of Orange. The violin sonatas (Opus 4; K 26–31) which had been commissioned by the royal family were also printed in The Hague.

Amsterdam, Utrecht, Brussels once more; Paris and Versailles; then on to Lyon (where the young Mozart witnessed a public execution); and finally Geneva, Bern,

Mozart bei Madame Pompadour
Kolorierter Holzstich, um 1890

Mozart at Mme. Pompadour's
Colored wood engraving, c. 1890

Mozart chez Madame de Pompadour
Gravure sur bois coloriée, vers 1890

Seite 19: Die Familie Mozart in Paris
Stich von J.-B. Delafosse, 1763

Page 19: The Mozart family in Paris
Engraving by J.-B. Delafosse, 1763

Page 19: La famille Mozart à Paris
Eau-forte de J.-B. Delafosse, 1763

Mozart als Attraktion einer Teegesell-
schaft beim Prinzen Louis-François de
Conti in Paris. Gemälde von Michel-Barthélemy Ollivier, 1766
Seite 22 oben: Titelblatt der 1765 in London als Opus 3 gedruckten sechs Sonaten für Klavier und Violine (Flöte) und
Violoncello (KV 10–15)
Seite 22 unten: Johann Christian Bach ist
der jüngste Sohn des legendären Leipzi-
ger Thomaskantors. Die Begegnung mit
dem Komponisten ist von einschneiden-
der Bedeutung für den jungen Mozart.
Porträt von Thomas Gainsborough, 1776
Seite 23: Mozart als Vierzehnjähriger.
Das Porträt von Saverio Della Rosa entstand im Januar 1770.

Mozart as the attraction at a tea party of
Louis-François de Conti's in Paris. Painting by Michel-Barthélemy Ollivier, 1766
Page 22, top: Title page of the collection
of six Sonatas for Piano and Violin (Flute)
and Cello (K 10–15), printed in London
as "Opus 3" in 1765
Page 22, bottom: Johann Christian Bach
(1735–1782) was the youngest son of the
legendary cantor of the St. Thomas'
Church in Leipzig, Germany. Mozart's
meeting with the composer had a decisive
influence on the young Mozart. Portrait
by Thomas Gainsborough, 1776
Page 23: Mozart as a fourteen-year-old
boy. The portrait by Saverio Della Rosa
was painted in January 1770.

Mozart, point de mire de l'assemblée
venue prendre le thé chez le prince Louis-
François de Conti à Paris. Tableau de
Michel-Barthélemy Ollivier, 1766
Page 22, en haut: Couverture de l'opus 3,
publié en 1765 à Londres et contenant
les partitions des six sonates pour piano
et violon (flûte) et violoncelle (K. 10–15).
Page 22, en bas: Johann Christian Bach,
le plus jeune fils du légendaire cantor à la
Thomasschule de Leipzig. Sa rencontre
avec le compositeur aura une importance
cruciale pour le jeune Mozart. Portrait de
Thomas Gainsborough, 1776
Page 23: Mozart à l'âge de quatorze ans.
Le portrait fut peint par Saverio Della
Rosa en janvier 1770.

Que Léopold à Paris ait mis la main à leur écriture
définitive et à leur mise au net est un fait certain, mais il
s'agit en réalité de compositions autonomes en soi,
enrichies seulement de quelques emprunts à des compositeurs issus du cercle des relations parisiennes.

Stimulé par les succès parisiens, Léopold s'attaque
à la seconde grande cible, Londres. Le 22 avril 1764, la
famille embarque à Calais pour une traversée en direction de l'Angleterre. Cinq jours plus tard, les enfants se
produisent pour la première fois devant le couple royal à
Buckingham House.

Le séjour londonien est probablement le chapitre le
plus excitant du voyage en Europe occidentale, car tout
en Angleterre est différent du continent: la société est
plus ouverte, les différences de rang ont moins d'importance, le capitalisme est florissant, même dans la vie
musicale. La ville dans laquelle ont été inventés les concerts par abonnements, est un lieu de prédilection des
artistes lyriques et des compositeurs étrangers, qui
trouvent leur public non seulement dans les théâtres et
les maisons particulières, mais aussi dans les jardins
publics. Parmi ces séries de concerts par abonnements,
une de celles qui ont le plus de succès a été créée par
Jean Christian Bach. Le benjamin des fils de Jean Sébas-
tien Bach ne compose pas seulement des opéras italiens,
mais également des symphonies et des concertos pour

Six
SONATES
pour le
CLAVECIN
qui peuvent se jouer avec
L'accompagnement de Violon ou Flaute
Traversiere
Très humblement dediées
A SA MAJESTE
CHARLOTTE
REINE de la GRANDE BRETAGNE
Composées par
I.G. WOLFGANG MOZART
Agé de huit Ans
Oeuvre III.

LONDON Printed for the Author and Sold at his Lodgings
Et M.r Williamson in Thrift Street Soho

piano, dont «l'allegro chantant» inspire le jeune Mozart. C'est dans les salles de Spring Garden et du Ranelagh que les enfants Mozart, que leur père fait toujours passer comme ayant un ou deux ans de moins que leur âge réel, font leur première grande apparition. La recette du premier concert représente l'équivalent de 800 florins, ce qui correspond à plus de deux années de traitement d'un musicien de la cour de Salzbourg. De telles circonstances font naître en Léopold des idées véritablement révolutionnaire : «C'est une bonne chose qu'ici le peuple et un bon millier d'honnêtes gens qui gagnent leur pain à la sueur de leur front, et qui constituent en fait l'Etat et maintiennent la cohésion de tout l'édifice civil, ne soient pas obligés de souffrir et de se consumer pour une petite centaine [...] qui passe sa vie dans l'opulence.» On n'a pas trace de termes plus explicites dans lesquels il exprimerait sa rébellion contre l'absolutisme et sa propre condition de laquais, car sur le chemin de la poste, cette lettre est tombée entre les mains de la censure. Dans la correspondance qu'échangeront par la suite le père et le fils, des choses confidentielles seront rédigées dans une écriture chiffrée.

Le 13 mai 1765, les deux enfants font encore une apparition publique avec, dit-on, la sonate pour piano à quatre mains en ré majeur (K. 19d), dont l'authenticité est du reste contestée. Après quoi il semblerait que l'intérêt pour les enfants prodiges retombe. Léopold se voit contraint de passer une annonce dans le «Public Advertiser» stipulant que «toute personne désireuse d'entendre les jeunes prodiges» en a la possibilité tous les après-midi de une heure à trois heures. Si en mai, il demande encore un droit d'entrée de cinq shillings par personne, celui-ci n'est plus que de deux shillings et six pence en juillet. A la fin du mois, il prend avec sa famille le bateau pour Calais, où il avait laissé la voiture de voyage, il la fait atteler et met le cap sur les grandes villes de Flandre et de Hollande, avec pour principal objectif La Haye. Il avait été invité à s'y rendre alors qu'il se trouvait encore en Angleterre par l'ambassadeur hollandais, le comte Jan Walraad Walderen.

La Hollande est l'un des grands centres d'édition musicale européens. La méthode de violon de Léopold Mozart paraît en néerlandais à Haarlem en 1766, dans une remarquable édition composée à partir de caractères typographiques et non plus en stéréotypie, comme c'était alors l'usage. Le prince Guillaume V d'Orange,

Amsterdam, Utrecht, noch einmal Brüssel, Paris und Versailles, danach Lyon (wo Mozart Zeuge einer öffentlichen Hinrichtung wird), schließlich Genf, Bern und Zürich sind die wichtigsten Stationen der sich über fast ein Jahr und mehr als zweitausend Kilometer hinziehenden Rückreise nach Salzburg, die sich krankheitsbedingt verzögert. Noch in Den Haag werden die Kinder von Bauchtyphus heimgesucht, Nannerl erkrankt so schwer, daß sie im Oktober 1765 die Sterbesakramente erhält; nach ihr wird der Bruder für mehrere Wochen bettlägerig. Auf der letzten Etappe, in München, meldet sich der Gelenkrheumatismus zurück – eine neuerliche Manifestation jener Krankheit, die als wahrscheinlichste Ursache für Mozarts frühen Tod zu gelten hat.

and Zurich—these were the most important stations that led the family back to Salzburg on a circuitous journey lasting almost a year and covering more than twelve hundred miles. Their return had been slowed by illness. While still in The Hague, the children had been beset by an intestinal typhus that nearly brought Nannerl to death's door: in October 1765 she was given the last rites of the church for the dying. On the heels of her crisis, Wolfgang was also confined to bed for several weeks. Finally, during the last stage of their journey, rheumatic fever struck the boy once more in Munich—a recurrence of the illness that was to be the most probable cause of his death a quarter of a century later.

alors âgé de dix-huit ans, en est du reste l'un des premiers propriétaires. Les sonates pour violon opus 4 (K. 26–31), issues d'une commande de la maison royale, paraissent à La Haye sous forme imprimée.

Amsterdam, Utrecht, Bruxelles à nouveau, Paris et Versailles, puis Lyon (où Mozart est témoin d'une exécution capitale publique), et enfin Genève, Berne et Zurich sont les étapes les plus importantes du retour à Salzbourg. Le voyage, qui s'échelonne sur presque un an et plus de deux mille kilomètres, traîne en longueur pour des raisons de santé. En effet, les enfants, alors qu'ils se trouvent encore à La Haye, sont victimes du typhus hépatique, et l'état de Nannerl est si grave qu'elle reçoit les derniers sacrements en octobre 1765 ; puis c'est au tour du frère de garder la chambre pendant plusieurs semaines. A Munich, la dernière étape, c'est un regain de rhumatismes articulaires qui s'annonce, nouvelle manifestation de cette maladie à laquelle on peut en toute vraisemblance imputer la mort prématurée de Mozart.

Mozart als Ritter vom Goldenen Sporn. Anonymes Gemälde (Kopie eines 1777 für den Freund und Förderer Padre Giovanni Battista Martini und die Akademie in Bologna angefertigten Porträts). Mozart erhielt diesen Orden von Papst Clemens XIV. im Jahr 1770 mit der Begründung, daß er sich von „frühester Jugend an in süßester Weise im Cembalospiel ausgezeichnet" habe. Die Ordensinsignien sind ein goldenes Kreuz am roten Band, Degen und Sporen. Zu den Höhepunkten des Rom-Aufenthalts gehört ein Besuch der Sixtinischen Kapelle, wo er das berühmte „Miserere" von Gregorio Allegri hört.
Seite 24: Innenansicht des Petersdoms in Rom. Gemälde von Giovanni Paolo Pannini, um 1750

Mozart as a Knight of the Golden Spur. Anonymous painting (copy of a portrait done in 1777 for Mozart's friend and patron, Padre Giovanni Battista Martini and the Bolognese Academy). Mozart received the nomination to the Order from Pope Clement XIV in 1770 on the ground that he had "from his earliest youth distinguished himself in the sweetest manner in playing the cembalo." The insignia of the Order consisted of a golden cross on a red band, a dagger and spurs. Among the highlights of Mozart's stay in Rome was a visit to the Sistine Chapel where the boy heard the famous "Misere" by Gregorio Allegri.
Page 24: Interior view of St. Peter's Cathedral in Rome. Painting by Giovanni Paolo Pannini, c. 1750

Mozart, chevalier de l'Eperon d'or. Peinture anonyme (copie d'un portrait réalisé en 1777 pour le Padre Giovanni Battista Martini, son ami et mécène, et pour l'Académie de Bologne). Mozart fut admis dans cet ordre par le pape Clément XIV en 1770 en raison «de la manière exquise dont il s'est distingué au clavecin depuis sa plus tendre enfance». Les insignes de l'Ordre sont une croix dorée attachée à un ruban rouge, une dague et des éperons. La visite de la chapelle Sixtine où il entendra le célèbre «Miserere» de Gregorio Allegri sera l'un des points forts du séjour à Rome.
Page 24: Saint-Pierre de Rome, vue intérieure. Tableau de Giovanni Paolo Pannini, vers 1750

Unterwegs zu neuen Zielen

On the Road to New Goals

Stand Mozarts kompositorisches Schaffen während der großen Westeuropareise im Zeichen der Orchester- und Kammermusik, die er in öffentlichen Konzerten präsentierte – nicht zuletzt, um für die Druckausgaben seiner Sonaten zu werben –, so stürzt er sich, in Salzburg angekommen, mit wahrem Feuereifer auf die dramatische Musik. Schon in einem Brief aus London, wo die Arie „Va, dal furor portata" (KV 21) entstanden war, hatte Leopold bemerkt, Wolfgang habe „ietzt immer eine opera im kopf, die er mit lauter jungen leuten in Salzburg aufführen will". Und in der Tat, das erste Werk, das nach der Ankunft in Salzburg entsteht, ist „Or che dover/Tali e cotanti sono" (KV 33), eine Tenor-Arie mit einleitendem Rezitativ; Trompeten verleihen ihr ein besonders festliches Gepräge – auch das ein Beweis gewachsener Souveränität, denn die Trompete ist ein Instrument, dessen Lautstärke Mozart als Kind immer gefürchtet hat. Uraufgeführt wird die Arie als Dreingabe zur Theateraufführung einer italienischen Schauspieltruppe, die auf Einladung des Fürsterzbischofs in Salzburg gastiert. Kaum ein halbes Jahr später folgt „Apollo et Hyacinthus" (KV 38), eine lateinische Schulkomödie, die am 13. Mai 1767 als musikalisch-szenische Einlage (Intermedium) zwischen den Akten einer

During their great western European tour, Mozart's compositional efforts had been directed to orchestral and chamber music which he then performed in public concerts—a good method of advertisement for the printed editions of his sonatas. Upon his return to Salzburg, however, he threw himself with fiery zeal into dramatic music. Even in London, where the boy had composed the aria "Va, dal furor portata" (K 21), Leopold had remarked in a letter that his son now had "his mind full of an opera that he wants to present it in Salzburg together with other young people." And in fact, the first work that Wolfgang composed after his arrival in his home city was "Or che dover / Tali e cotanti sono" (K 33), a tenor aria with an introductory recitative. The use of trumpets not only lent the work an especially solemn character, but also indicated Mozart's increasing maturity, for as a child, he had been afraid of the instrument's loud blare. The aria was first presented as an encore in a theatrical performance by a troupe of Italian actors who were guests of the prince-archbishop of Salzburg. Scarcely half a year later, Mozart composed "Apollo et Hyacinthus" (K 38), a Latin school-comedy, first presented on May 13, 1767, to students in the auditorium of the University of Salzburg as a musical-scenic interlude

Paris ce 3 juillet 1778

...sten Tag in meinem Leben ..., meine Mutter,

Ausschnitt aus Mozarts Brief an Abbé
Bullinger vom 3. Juli 1778, geschrieben
am Todestag der Mutter in Paris:
„Trauern Sie mit mir mein Freund! –
Dies war der traurigste Tag in meinem
Leben ..." Bei dem Porträt handelt es
sich um eine 1777 entstandene Miniatur
aus Elfenbein.

Excerpt from Mozart's letter to Abbé
Bullinger, written on 3 July, 1778, the day
of his mother's death in Paris. "Grieve
with me, my friend!—This was the sad-
dest day of my life ..." The portrait is an
ivory miniature painted in 1777.

Extrait de la lettre de Mozart à l'abbé
Bullinger, le 3 juillet 1778, date du décès
de sa mère à Paris : « Joignez-vous à ma
tristesse mon ami ! – Ce fut le plus triste
jour de ma vie... » Le portrait est une
miniature en ivoire réalisée en 1777.

A la conquête de nouveaux objectifs

Si pendant le grand voyage en Europe occidentale, les
compositions de Mozart – qu'il présentait à l'occasion
de concerts publics auxquels le souci de promouvoir les
éditions imprimées de ses sonates n'était pas étranger –
étaient placées sous le signe de la musique symphonique et de la musique de chambre, il se précipite avec
fougue sur la musique dramatique dès son arrivée à
Salzbourg. A Londres, où avait été composé l'air «Va, dal
furor portata» (K. 21), Léopold avait déjà remarqué dans
une lettre que Wolfgang avait «à présent toujours un
opéra en tête et qu'il veut le monter à Salzbourg avec
uniquement des jeunes gens». Et la première œuvre
qu'il crée après son retour à Salzbourg est en effet «Or
che dover / Tali e cotanti sono» (K. 33), un air de ténor
précédé d'un récitatif auquel les trompettes donnent un
accent particulièrement solennel – ce qui par ailleurs
représente une preuve d'évolution et de maturité, car la
trompette est un instrument dont la puissance sonore a
toujours effrayé Mozart enfant. L'air est chanté pour la
première fois à l'occasion d'une représentation théâtrale, à laquelle il vient s'ajouter. La représentation est
donnée par une troupe de comédiens italiens qui, à
l'invitation du prince-archevêque, se produisent à Salzbourg. L'œuvre est suivie à peine six mois plus tard de la

Tragödie vor Studenten in der Aula der Salzburger Universität erklingt: Mozarts erster kleiner Beitrag zur Gattung Oper.

Durch die hoffnungsvollen Gehversuche auf dem noch ungewohnten Terrain rücken Wien und Italien ins Blickfeld. Dort, wo der Stern der Oper am hellsten strahlt, winken Ruhm, Ehre und beträchtliche Einnahmen. Es gilt, die Zinsen der gewaltigen Summen einzufahren, die Leopold Mozart in die Zukunft seines Sohnes investiert hat. Eine ›scrittura‹, einen Opernauftrag, zu erhalten, ist das nächste große Ziel, und in Wien scheint es zum Greifen nah. Dort steht im September 1767 eine kaiserliche Hochzeitsfeier an, zu der die Familie Mozart geschlossen anreist. Aber die Vermählung findet nicht statt, denn die 16jährige Braut, Erzherzogin Maria Josepha, wird Opfer der in Wien grassierenden Blattern-Epidemie. Die Mozarts reisen nach Mähren, um der Ansteckungsgefahr zu entgehen, doch Wolfgang ist schon infiziert. Ende Oktober brechen die Pocken zuerst bei ihm, danach bei Nannerl aus. Sein Gesicht bleibt von der Krankheit gezeichnet. Erst Anfang 1767 kehrt er mit der Familie aus Olmütz nach Wien zurück und wird am Hof empfangen.

Joseph II., der nachmalige Kaiser und Mitregent Maria Theresias seit 1765, schlägt ihm tatsächlich vor, eine komische Oper zu komponieren, doch kann auch er die Aufführung des schon im Sommer 1768 fertiggestellten Werks („La finta semplice" KV 51) nicht gegen Giuseppe Affligio durchsetzen, den neuen Pächter des Burgtheaters. Leopold Mozart glaubt an eine Verschwörung, wahrscheinlich aber scheute Affligio nur das Risiko, die Geschicke seines Hauses, wenn auch nur vorübergehend, in die Hände eines Zwölfjährigen zu legen.

(Intermedium) between the acts of a tragedy. This was Mozart's first small contribution to the operatic genre.

These promising first steps into unfamiliar artistic territory brought both Vienna and Italy into focus. There, where the star of the opera stood at the zenith, the promise of fame, honor, and considerable income beckoned—money that would serve as repayment for the enormous sums Leopold Mozart had invested in his son's future. Obtaining a *scrittura*, or commission for an opera, became their next great goal, and Vienna promised fair to bring that dream within reach, for in September 1767 an imperial wedding was to take place. Once again the Mozart family journeyed as a body to Vienna, but the marriage was never celebrated, for the sixteen-year-old bride, Archduchess Maria Josepha, fell victim to the smallpox epidemic raging through the city at the time. To escape contagion, the Mozarts departed for Moravia, but to no avail: Wolfgang was already infected. At the end of October, the first pocks appeared, and soon Nannerl fell ill too. Mozart's face retained the scars of the disease ever after. Not until the beginning of 1767 did the family return from Olmütz (today Olmouc) to Vienna, where they were welcomed by the court.

Joseph II, co-regent with Maria Theresia since 1765 and later emperor, in fact proposed that Mozart write a comic opera. The result was "La finta semplice" (K 51, The dissembled simplicity), which he finished in the summer of 1768. But even the king was not able to enforce his will for staging the boy's work against that of Giuseppe Affligio, the new leaseholder of the Burgtheater. Leopold Mozart suspected intrigue, but it is more probable that Affligio feared to risk the fate of his house, even temporarily, in the hands of a twelve-year-old. The

28

comédie « Apollon et Hyacinthe » (K. 38), un exercice de
style écrit en latin qui sera créé devant un public d'étu-
diants le 13 mai 1767 dans la salle d'honneur de l'université de Salzbourg, où il fait office d'intermède musical et
scénique entre les actes d'une tragédie. Il s'agit là de la
première contribution de Mozart au genre lyrique.

Avec ces premiers pas prometteurs sur un terrain
encore peu familier, les regards vont désormais se
tourner vers Vienne et l'Italie. Ces pôles où l'étoile de
l'opéra rayonne avec le maximum d'intensité font en
effet miroiter gloire, honneurs et confortables rentrées
d'argent. Il s'agit à présent de recueillir les intérêts des
énormes sommes que Léopold Mozart a investies dans
l'avenir de son rejeton. Obtenir une « scrittura », une
commande d'opéra, est le prochain grand objectif, et à
Vienne, il semble bien près d'y réussir. Il est en effet
prévu d'y célébrer en septembre 1767 un mariage
impérial, auquel la famille Mozart se rend au grand
complet. Mais les épousailles n'ont finalement pas lieu,
car la mariée, l'archiduchesse Marie Joséphine, âgée de
seize ans, est victime de l'épidémie de variole qui sévit
alors à Vienne. Les Mozart partent pour Mähren dans
l'espoir d'échapper à la contagion, mais Wolfgang est
déjà contaminé. C'est d'abord chez lui qu'apparaissent
les pustules, en octobre, puis chez Nannerl. Son visage
restera marqué par la maladie. Ce n'est que début 1767
qu'il quitte Olmütz avec sa famille pour repartir à
Vienne, où il est reçu à la cour.

Joseph II, le futur empereur qui pour l'instant
partage la régence avec Marie-Thérèse depuis 1765, lui
propose effectivement de composer un opéra bouffe.
Mais bien que l'œuvre soit terminée dès l'été 1768
(« La finta semplice », K. 51), il ne parvient pas à
imposer sa représentation à Giuseppe Affligio, le
nouveau directeur du Burgtheater. Léopold Mozart
croit à un complot, alors qu'Affligio redoutait vraisemblablement de remettre, même à titre provisoire, le
destin de sa maison entre les mains d'un gamin de
douze ans. Il est tout de même réconfortant pour
Mozart de voir qu'une représentation privée de son
petit *singspiel* « Bastien et Bastienne » (K. 50) est
donnée dans le pavillon du jardin du riche médecin et
magnétiseur Franz Anton Mesmer. Quant à la création
avortée de « La finta semplice » (La fausse innocence),
elle finit par se faire à Salzbourg le 1ᵉʳ mai 1769, en
l'honneur du comte de Schrattenbach.

Angebliches Porträt Mozarts. Gouache
von Johann Nepomuk Della Croce,
um 1780
Seite 28: Ansicht der Stadt und des
Schlosses von Mannheim. Kolorierter
Kupferstich von Hieronymus Wolff nach
Friedrich Bernhard Werner, 1729

Presumed portrait of Mozart. Gouache
by Johann Nepomuk Della Croce, c. 1780.
Page 28: City and palace of Mannheim.
Colored copperplate engraving by
Hieronymus Wolff from an original by
Friedrich Bernhard Werner, 1729

Portrait présumé de Mozart. Gouache de
Johann Nepomuk Della Croce, vers 1780
Page 28 : Mannheim, vue de la ville et du
château. Eau-forte coloriée de Hiero-
nymus Wolff d'après Friedrich Bernhard
Werner, 1729

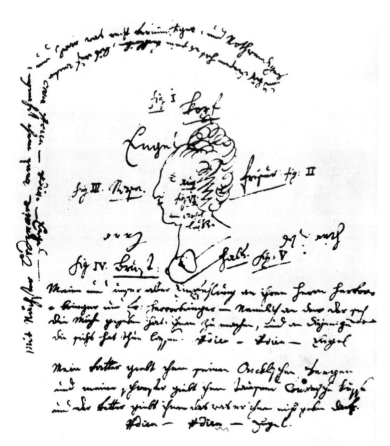

Tröstlich für Mozart, daß wenigstens im Gartenpavillon des wohlhabenden Mediziners und Magnetiseurs Franz Anton Mesmer („Mesmerismus") eine Privataufführung des kleinen Singspiels „Bastien und Bastienne" (KV 50) zustandekommt. Die geplatzte Uraufführung der „Finta semplice" (Die verstellte Einfalt) wird am 1. Mai 1769 zu Ehren Graf Schrattenbachs in Salzburg nachgeholt.

Verärgert über Leopold Mozarts Urlaubsübertretung hatte der Fürsterzbischof die Bezüge seines Vizekapellmeisters einbehalten, doch als es im Herbst wieder auf die Reise geht, diesmal nach Italien, steuert er 120 Dukaten (540 Gulden) aus seiner Privatschatulle bei. Auf dieser ersten und mit fünfzehn Monaten Dauer längsten der drei Italienreisen, die Mozart zwischen 1769 und 1773 mit seinem Vater unternimmt, scheinen alle Träume wahr zu werden. In Mailand mit großen Opern-

young composer, however, was at least able console himself with a private performance of the small Singspiel "Bastien und Bastienne" (K 50) that was staged in the garden pavilion of the wealthy doctor and magnetizer Franz Anton Mesmer (discoverer of mesmerism, or hypnotism). The family was rewarded for the thwarted premier of "Finta semplice" when it was produced in honor of Count Schrattenbach in Salzburg on May 1, 1769.

The prince-archbishop, annoyed at Leopold Mozart's overextended leave, had meanwhile suspended the salary of his vice-orchestra director. Nonetheless, when the Mozarts once again set off in the autumn, this time to Italy, he donated 120 ducats (540 gulden) from his private funds. For the next fifteen months, on this first and longest of the three Italian tours that Mozart undertook with his father between 1769 and 1773, it

Ansicht Münchens im 19. Jahrhundert. Kolorierter Stahlstich, anonym, um 1850. Zur Vorbereitung der für den 22. Januar angesetzten und schließlich noch um eine Woche verschobenen Premiere des „Idomeneo" hält Mozart sich seit November 1780 in München auf. Den ihm für die Einstudierung und Aufführung gewährten Urlaub von sechs Wochen dehnt er auf vier Monate aus.
Seite 32: Längsschnitt durch den Zuschauerraum des von François Cuvilliés erbauten Residenztheaters in München, Uraufführungsort des „Idomeneo". Kupferstich von Valerian Funck, 1771. Eine technische Besonderheit stellt der auf Bühnenniveau anhebbare Boden des Zuschauerraums dar. Das Gebäude selbst existiert nicht mehr, aber die kostbare Innenausstattung wurde vor der Zerstörung im Zweiten Weltkrieg bewahrt.

Ninetheenth-century view of Munich. Anonymous colored steel plate engraving, c. 1850. In preparation for the premier of "Idomeneo," scheduled for January 22, but in the end postponed a week, Mozart had been in Munich since November 1780, thus stretching the leave of absence that had been granted him for the rehersal and performance of the opera from six weeks to four months.
Page 32: Cut-away view of the auditorium of the palace theater in Munich, built by François Cuvilliés. Here "Idomeneo" was first performed. Copper plate engraving by Valerian Funck, 1771. A special technical feature was the moveable floor of the audience area which could be raised to the level of the stage. The original building has not survived, but the precious interior equipment and decoration were saved from the destruction of World War II.

Munich au 19e siècle. Gravure sur métal coloriée, anonyme, vers 1850. Mozart se trouve depuis le mois de novembre 1780 à Munich pour préparer la première d'«Idoménée» fixée le 22 janvier et qui sera finalement repoussée d'une semaine. Il prolongera jusqu'à quatre mois le congé de six semaines qui lui a été accordé pour étudier et présenter l'opéra.
Page 32: Coupe longitudinale de la salle de spectacle du Residenztheater édifié par François Cuvilliés à Munich et où sera jouée la première d'«Idoménée». Eau-forte de Valerian Funck, 1771. Particularité d'ordre technique: le sol de la salle peut être soulevé jusqu'au niveau de la scène. Le bâtiment lui-même n'existe plus mais les meubles et la décoration intérieure de grande valeur ont pu être préservés de la destruction pendant la Deuxième Guerre mondiale.

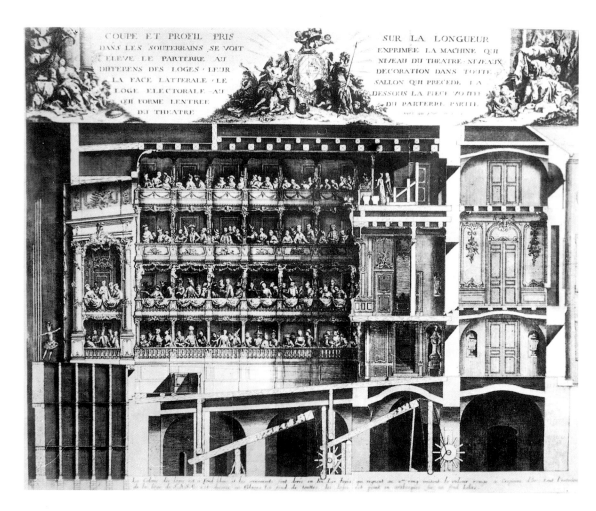

auträgen geehrt, im Vatikan zum Ritter vom Goldenen Sporn geadelt, in Bologna zum Mitglied der ehrwürdigen „Accademia filarmonica" ernannt, enteilt er mit Riesenschritten seiner Kindheit und steht mit fünfzehn Jahren fast auf einer Stufe mit Komponisten wie Johann Adolf Hasse oder Christoph Willibald Gluck. Aber auch dieser frühe Ruhm verblaßt, genauso wie der Zauber, der das einstige Wunderkind umgab. In Salzburg, wohin er nur zurückkehrt, weil sich die Hoffnungen auf eine feste Anstellung in Italien zerschlagen, nimmt er den Rang eines unbesoldeten dritten Konzertmeisters ein; 1772 gewährt ihm Graf Colloredo, Schrattenbachs Nachfolger, ein Gehalt von bescheidenen 150 Gulden jährlich.

seemed that all their dreams were coming true: In Milan, Mozart received large opera commissions, in Rome he was dubbed a Knight of the Golden Spur, and in Bologna he was named member of the venerable *Accademia filamonica*. He left his childhood swiftly behind, and at age fifteen stood almost on an equal level with composers like Johann Adolf Hasse and Christoph Willibald Gluck. But as in London, this early fame soon paled, along with the luster that once surrounded the former Wunderkind. In Salzburg, where he returned only when hopes for a permanent appointment in Italy had been dashed, Wolfgang accepted the position of unpaid third *Konzertmeister*. In 1772 Graf Colloredo, Schrattenbach's successor, granted him a modest salary of 150 gulden annually.

Irrité par Léopold Mozart qui n'avait pas respecté la durée de son congé, le prince-archevêque avait procédé à une retenue sur les émoluments de son vice-maître de chapelle, mais quand celui-ci, l'automne venu, se prépare à entreprendre un nouveau périple en direction cette fois de l'Italie, il lui fait don de 120 ducats (540 florins) prélevés sur sa cassette personnelle. Au cours des quinze mois qui font de ce premier voyage le plus long des trois voyages en Italie entrepris par Mozart, en compagnie de son père, entre 1769 et 1773, tous les rêves semblent devenir réalité. Honoré d'importantes commandes à Milan, promu chevalier de l'Eperon d'Or au Vatican, nommé membre de la respectable « Accademia filarmonica » à Bologne, il sort de l'enfance à pas de géants et à quinze ans, il se retrouve presque sur le même plan que des compositeurs comme Johann Adolf Hasse ou Christoph Willibald Gluck. Mais cette gloire précoce pâlit elle aussi comme avait pâli la magie qui entourait l'enfant prodige d'autrefois. A Salzbourg, où il ne revient que parce que se sont effondrées ses espérances d'obtenir une place fixe en Italie, il occupe sans rémunération aucune le rang de troisième maître de concert ; en 1772, le comte de Colloredo, le successeur de Schrattenbach, lui alloue un traitement annuel de 150 florins.

IDOMENEO.
DRAMMA
PER
MUSICA
DA RAPPRESENTARSI
NEL TEATRO NUOVO DI
CORTE
PER COMANDO
DI S. A. S E.
CARLO TEODORO
Come Palatino del Rheno, Duca dell'
alta, e bafsa Baviera, e del Palatinato
Superiore, etc. etc. Archidapifero,
et Elettore, etc. etc.
NEL CARNOVALE
1781.

La Poesia è del Signor Abate Giambattista Varesco
Capellano di Corte di S. A. R. l'Arcivescovo, e Principe di Salisburgo.
La Musica è del Signor Maestro Wolfgango Amadeo Mozart Academico di Bologna, e di Verona, in fin attual servizio di S. A. R. l'Arcivescovo, e Principe di Salisburgo.
La Traduzione è del Signor Andrea Schachtner, pure in attual servizio di S. A. R. l'Arcivescovo, e Principe di Salisburgo.

MONACO.
Aprefso Francesco Giuseppe Thuille.

Oben: Titelblatt des „Idomeneo"-Textbuchs, 1781
Rechts: Salzburg, Mozartplatz (vormals Michaelsplatz). Anonymes Gemälde aus der 2. Hälfte des 18. Jahrhunderts

Top: Title page of the libretto of "Idomeneo," 1781
Right: Salzburg, Mozartplatz (formerly Michaelsplatz). Anonymous painting from the second half of the 18th century

Ci-dessus : Couverture du livret d'« Idoménée », 1781
A droite : Salzbourg, Mozartplatz (anciennement Michaelsplatz). Peinture anonyme de la seconde moitié du 18ᵉ siècle

Abschied von Salzburg

Die italienischen Erfolge liegen schon fünf Jahre zurück, als Mozart im Herbst 1777 erneut versucht, dem ungeliebten Salzburger Hofdienst, der Langeweile, die ihn umgibt, und der kompositorischen Routine zu entfliehen. Diesmal begleitet ihn die Mutter, denn Leopold kann bei Urlaubsgesuchen nicht länger auf das Entgegenkommen seines Dienstherrn rechnen. Es ist eine Bewerbungsreise in der letzten Endes vergeblichen Hoffnung auf einen Opernauftrag oder eine angemessener bezahlte Anstellung in Deutschland. Nachgerade zynisch muß es Mozart erscheinen, daß Kurfürst Maximilian III. Joseph ihm rät, er solle „nach Italien reisen, sich berühmt machen", ehe er eine Anstellung in München anstrebe. Auch in Mannheim bietet sich wenig Aussicht auf Beschäftigung. Der Freundschaft zu den Musikern des berühmten Orchesters wegen, aber auch aus Liebe zur siebzehnjährigen Sängerin Aloisia Weber, die er in Mannheim kennenlernt, bleibt Mozart länger als notwendig dort. Als Leopold davon erfährt, befiehlt er, die „Narrenspossen" zu beenden: „Fort mit Dir nach Paris!"

Im März 1778 treffen Mozart und seine Mutter nach einer zehntägigen Wagenfahrt durch Hitze, Sturm und Regen in der französischen Hauptstadt ein. Um die Reise zu finanzieren, hatten sie den eigenen, sechzehn Jahre alten Wagen verkauft, mit der Bedingung, daß der Käufer, ein Fuhrunternehmer, sie noch nach Paris kutschierte. Auch diese Reise wird zum Fehlschlag, ja zur Tragödie. Am 3. Juli stirbt, 58jährig, seine Mutter, und Mozart findet nicht den Mut, es dem Vater mitzuteilen. Er schaltet einen Freund der Familie ein, Abbé Bullinger, der die Todesnachricht überbringen soll. Doch Leopold hat die Wahrheit längst erraten und hadert nun mit seinem Sohn, den er verdächtigt, die Mutter um des eigenen Fortkommens willen vernachlässigt zu haben. Der Vorwurf bleibt zunächst unausgesprochen, aber dann heißt es in einem Brief: „Wäre Deine Mutter von Mannheim nach Salzburg zurückgekommen, so würde sie nicht gestorben sein."

Als Gescheiterter kehrt Mozart heim und bittet den verhaßten Erzbischof untertänigst um Wiederaufnahme in die Hofkapelle. Schwerpunkt seiner Tätigkeit in Salz-

Farewell to Salzburg

With his Italian successes already five years behind him, Mozart tried once again in 1777 to escape from the irksome duties, boredom, and routine compositional work that were his lot at the Salzburg court. This time, the young man was accompanied by his mother, for Leopold could no longer expect his overlord to look with favor upon yet another application for leave of duty. It was to be a promotional tour, undertaken in the hope—which in the end proved futile—of obtaining a commission for an opera or an appropriately paid appointment in Germany. It must have seemed nothing less than cynical to Mozart when the Elector Maximillian III Joseph recommended that he "travel to Italy to make himself famous" rather than aspire to a position in Munich. In Mannheim, too, there was little hope of employment. Partly out of friendship with the musicians of the famous orchestra, but also for love of the seventeen-year-old singer Aloisia Weber, whom he met in Mannheim, Mozart lingered longer than business required. When Leopold heard of this, he demanded that the "fools' farce" come to an end: "Get yourself on to Paris."

In March 1778, Mozart and his mother finally arrived in the French capital after a ten-day carriage ride through heat, wind and rain. To pay for the journey, they had sold their sixteen-year-old "family carriage" under the condition that the buyer, a haulage contractor, drive them to Paris. But this journey also proved to be a mistake, even a tragedy. On July 3, Mozart's mother died, age 58, and the young man could not find the courage to inform his father. He appealed to a friend of the family in Salzburg, Abbé Bullinger, who was to break the news of the death. But Leopold had already long guessed the truth, and quarreled with his son, who he suspected had neglected his mother for the sake of his own advancement. At first the accusation remained unspoken, but a letter brought the suspicion to light: "If your mother had come back from Mannheim to Salzburg, she would not have died." Mozart returned in failure to Salzburg and bid the hated archbishop most humbly for reinstatement in the *Hofkapelle*.

Mozart's main activity in Salzburg, where he now filled the position of court organist at 450 gulden per

Anficht des Kohlmarkts   *Vuë du Kohlmarkt.*

Der Wiener Kohlmarkt und die St. Michaelskirche (rechts). Aquatinta von Karl Schütz, 1786. Nur für kurze Zeit, von Februar bis April 1783, bewohnt Mozart mit seiner schwangeren Frau „ein schlechtes Logis auf dem Kohlenmarkt Nr. 7". Es ist die fünfte seiner insgesamt 13 Wohnungen in Wien, die meisten davon zentral gelegen, d. h. innerhalb des heutigen Ersten Bezirks.

The Vienna Kohlmarkt and St. Michael's Church (right). Aquatint by Karl Schütz, 1786. For a short time, from February to April 1783, Mozart and his pregnant wife lived in "poor lodgings at Kohlenmarkt No. 7," the fifth of his altogether thirteen apartments in the city. Most of them were centrally located, i. e., within the present-day First District.

Le Kohlmarkt de Vienne et l'église Saint-Michel (à droite). Aquatinte de Karl Schütz, 1786. Pendant un bref moment, de février à avril 1783, Mozart et sa femme enceinte habitent dans «un mauvais logis, au 7 du Kohlmarkt». C'est le cinquième de ses treize logements à Vienne, la plupart situés au centre, c'est-à-dire à l'intérieur du premier arrondissement actuel.

Les adieux à Salzbourg

Les succès italiens remontent déjà à cinq ans lorsque Mozart, à l'automne 1777, tente une nouvelle fois d'échapper à ce service de la cour de Salzbourg qu'il a en horreur. Sa mère cette fois l'accompagne, car Léopold ne peut plus compter sur la complaisance de son patron pour prétendre à un congé. Ce voyage est entrepris avec l'espoir d'obtenir une commande pour un opéra ou de postuler en Allemagne à une place mieux payée. Mozart doit ressentir le conseil que lui donne le prince électeur Maximilien III Joseph de « se rendre d'abord célèbre en Italie » avant d'aspirer à un poste à Munich, comme foncièrement cynique. Rares également sont les perspectives d'emploi à Mannheim. Son amitié pour les musiciens de cet orchestre réputé, mais aussi son amour pour la cantatrice de dix-sept ans Aloysia Weber, qu'il rencontre à Mannheim, le font demeurer dans cette ville plus longtemps que nécessaire. Quand Léopold apprend cela, il lui ordonne de mettre un terme à ces « bouffonneries » : « Fiche le camp à Paris ! »

Après dix jours de route, Mozart et sa mère arrivent en mars 1778 dans la capitale française. Mais ce voyage est lui aussi un échec, voire même une tragédie. Le 3 juillet, la mère meurt à l'âge de 58 ans. Mozart, qui ne trouve pas le courage d'annoncer la nouvelle à son père, en charge l'abbé Bullinger, un ami de la famille. Mais Léopold a depuis longtemps deviné la vérité et s'en prend à présent à son fils, dont il soupçonne qu'il a négligé sa mère pour s'occuper de sa carrière. Ce reproche, qui d'abord est tu, s'exprime ensuite dans une lettre : « Si ta mère était rentrée à Salzbourg après Mannheim, elle ne serait pas morte. »

C'est le profil bas que Mozart revient à Salzbourg où il demande très humblement à cet archevêque abhorré de le reprendre dans la chapelle princière. Il y occupe le poste d'organiste de la cour, ce qui lui vaut un traitement de 450 florins, et concentre dorénavant son activité sur la musique sacrée. Mais ses aspirations, elles, sont d'une toute autre nature, ce qui transparaît ici et là dans ses compositions liturgiques comme la Missa Solemnis (K. 337) et la fameuse Messe du Couronnement (K. 317), toutes deux en ut majeur. Il s'agit là d'œuvres qui, surtout en ce qui concerne la richesse de l'instrumentation, satis-

Joseph Haydn (1732–1809), der Kollege und väterliche Freund, dem Mozart in seinen Streichquartetten nacheifert. Gouache von Johann Zitterer, um 1795
Seite 36: Konstanze Mozart (1763–1842), geb. Weber. Gemälde von Hans Hansen, 1802

Joseph Haydn (1732–1809), colleague and fatherly friend, whom Mozart emulated in his string quartets. Gouache by Johann Zitterer, c. 1795
Page 36: Constanze Mozart (1763–1842), née Weber. Painting by Hans Hansen, 1802

Joseph Haydn (1732–1809), le collègue et ami paternel, que Mozart cherche à égaler dans ses quatuors à cordes. Gouache de Johann Zitterer, vers 1795
Page 36 : Constance Mozart (1763–1842), née Weber. Tableau de Hans Hansen, 1802

Lorenzo Da Ponte wird am 1. März 1783 von Joseph II.
zum Dichter des italienischen Theaters am Wiener
Hof ernannt. Für Mozart schreibt er die Libretti zu
„Figaro", „Don Giovanni" und „Così". Stich von
Michele Pekinino, um 1820
Seite 39: Der reformfreudige Kaiser Joseph II. ist
einer der wichtigsten Förderer Mozarts. Gemälde
von M. D. Oppenheim, 1840

Lorenzo Da Ponte was appointed poet to the Italian
theater at the Viennese court in March 1, 1783, and
wrote the librettos to "Figaro," "Don Giovanni" and
"Così" for Mozart. Engraving by M. Pekinino, c. 1820
Page 39: Reform-minded Emperor Joseph II was
one of Mozart's most important supporters.
Painting by M. D. Oppenheim, 1840

Le 1ᵉʳ mars 1783, Joseph II nomme Lorenzo Da Ponte
poète officiel du théâtre italien à la cour de Vienne.
Celui-ci écrit pour Mozart les livrets de « Figaro », de
« Don Giovanni » et de « Così ». Gravure de Michele
Pekinino, vers 1820
Page 39 : Joseph II est l'un des soutiens essentiels de
Mozart. Tableau de M. D. Oppenheim, 1840

burg, wo er nun das Amt eines Hoforganisten mit
450 Gulden jährlich versieht, ist die Kirchenmusik. Sein
Ehrgeiz freilich geht in eine andere Richtung, und das
schimmert auch durch seine Meßkompositionen wie die
Missa solemnis (KV 337) und die sogenannte Krönungsmesse (KV 317), beide in C-Dur, hindurch. Es sind Werke, die vor allem hinsichtlich der opulenten Orchesterbesetzung den Anspüchen an eine repäsentative Musik
für hohe kirchliche Feiertage Genüge tun und doch nur
etwa dreißig Minuten einschließlich der obligatorischen
Instrumentaleinlage (‚Epistelsonate') dauern. Colloredo
wünscht es so. Für Mozart ist es eine Gratwanderung,
den Eindruck allzu verweltlichter Musik zu vermeiden,
ohne seine Opernambitionen zu verleugnen. Das Ergeb-
nis sind Kompositionen von ungeheurer Dichte und
expressiver Spannung, gebändigt durch eine ausgefeilte,
nachgerade altmeisterliche Satztechnik (Kontrapunkt,
Fuge), ein Stil, der auf engstem Raum monumentale
Wirkungen und Momente größter Innigkeit erschafft.
Auch noch in späteren Jahren hat Mozart diese Messen
sehr geschätzt, ablesbar an Motiven und melodischen
Wendungen, die er aus dem Agnus Dei beider Werke in
seine Wiener Opern „Figaro" und „Così" übernimmt,
aber auch daran, daß er 1790 im Rahmen der Krönungs-
feierlichkeiten für Leopold II. noch einmal auf sie
zurückgreift.

Dennoch, die Zeit seit seiner Rückkehr aus Paris
ist ein einziges Warten auf den nächsten Opernauftrag.
Kartenspielen wird zu einer seiner Hauptbeschäftigun-
gen in Salzburg. Erst im Sommer 1780 winkt die Erlö-
sung: „Idomeneo, Rè di Creta" (KV 366) heißt das
Libretto, das er für die Münchner Karnevalssaison 1781
vertonen soll.

Die großen Chorszenen und die starke Verklammerung der Arien mit dem Bühnengeschehen verraten
Mozarts selbstbewußten Umgang mit der herkömm-
lichen ‚Opera seria' und ihrer starren Abfolge von Ge-
sangs‚nummern'. Trotzdem bleibt „Idomeneo" eine
Oper traditionellen Zuschnitts mit einer Kastratenpartie
für die zweite männliche Hauptrolle, obwohl die Zeit der
Kastraten und der barocken Ästhetik absoluter Künst-
lichkeit und Stilisierung eigentlich vorbei ist. Die Titel-
partie schreibt Mozart für den Tenor Anton Raaff, einen
alternden Star, den er noch von seinem Besuch am
pfalzbayrischen Hof in Mannheim kennt.

year, was church music. But his ambitions clearly lay in another direction, whose tones gleamed also through the masses he composed, such as the "Missa solemnis" (K 37) and the so-called "Coronation" Mass ("Krönungsmesse", K 317), both written in C- Minor. Particularly in the size of the orchestra they demand, these works provided the solemn and impressive music required for high church holy days, and yet are only about thirty minutes long, including the obligatory instrumental epistle sonata, for Colloredo demanded works of singularly compact brevity. Mozart thus walked the tightrope between avoiding the impression of all-too worldly music without renouncing his operatic ambitions. The resulting compositions are of extreme density and expressive tension, linked together through a polished mastery of traditional "learned" compositional technique (counterpoint and fugue)—a style that achieves both a monumental effect within the narrowest of confines and moments of great tenderness. Even in later years, Mozart continued to value these works, as evidenced not only in the motifs and melodic expressions that he borrowed from the "Agnus Dei" of both masses for his Vienna operas "Figaro" and "Così", but also in his appropriation of elements from these early works in 1790, on the occasion of the coronation ceremonies for Leopold II.

In spite of this productivity, in the period following his return from Paris, Mozart waited with single-minded hope for the next operatic commission. Card playing developed into one of his main pastimes in Salzburg. Not until the summer of 1780 did redemption beckon. Mozart was commissioned to set a libretto to music for the 1781 Carnival season in Munich; the name of the libretto was "Idomeneo, Rè de Creta" (K 366).

The large choral scenes and the close intertwining of the arias and the activity on stage reveal Mozart's self-confidence in dealing with the traditional *opera seria* and its rigid sequence of song "numbers." Nonetheless, "Idomeneo" remains an opera in the traditional mold, containing a castrato part for the second male role, even though the day of the castrati and the baroque aesthetic ideal of absolute artifice and stylization was in reality passé. Mozart wrote the title role for the tenor Anton Raaff, an aging star whom he knew from his visit to the court of the Bavarian Palatinate in Mannheim.

font aux exigences d'une musique destinée aux grandes fêtes religieuses mais qui curieusement ne durent qu'une trentaine de minutes, y compris l'intermède instrumental obligé («sonate de l'épître»). Tel est le désir de Colloredo. Eviter de donner à sa musique des accents trop profanes sans pour autant renier ses ambitions lyriques, voilà qui représente pour Mozart un périlleux exercice d'équilibre. Le résultat se traduit par des œuvres d'une densité extrême et d'une tension dans l'expression que tempère une technique de composition parfaitement maîtrisée et tout à fait digne des maîtres anciens (contrepoint, fugue). Mozart a toujours beaucoup aimé ces messes dont il reprendra, des années plus tard, des motifs et des tournures musicales, dans les opéras viennois «Figaro» et «Così» tout d'abord, où l'on entend des réminiscences des deux «Agnus Dei», en 1790 ensuite, dans le cadre des cérémonies du couronnement de Léopold II.

Pourtant, depuis son retour de Paris, ses jours ne se passent que dans l'attente de la commande d'un nouvel opéra. Jouer aux cartes devient une de ses occupations salzbourgeoises majeures. Ce n'est qu'au cours de l'été 1780 que sonne la délivrance. «Idoménée, Roi de Crète» (K. 366), tel est le titre du livret qu'il doit mettre en musique pour la saison 1781 du carnaval de Munich.

On reconnaît à l'importance de la participation du chœur et aux airs qui «collent» très fortement à l'action dramatique la connaissance très approfondie qu'avait Mozart de l'«opera seria» et de sa succession rigide de «numéros» chantés. «Idoménée» reste tout de même un opéra de facture traditionnelle avec sa partie de castrat pour le second rôle masculin, bien que l'époque des castrats et de l'esthétique baroque soit en réalité révolue. Mozart écrit la partie du rôle-titre pour le ténor Anton Raaff, une star vieillissante qu'il a connue au cours de sa visite à la cour de Mannheim.

Theaterbilderbogen mit Figurinen zu
„Die Entführung aus dem Serail", Berlin,
um 1829

Theatrical broadsheet with figures from
"Die Entführung aus dem Serail," Berlin,
c. 1829

Album d'illustrations de théâtre avec des
personnages de «L'Enlèvement au
sérail», Berlin, vers 1829

Bassa Selim.

N° 20 Pedrillo.

nze.   *Belmonte.*   *Blondchen.*   *Osmin.*

ave.   *Stummer!*   *Türkische Officiere.*

bei Winckelmann & Söhne in Berlin.

Idealisierendes Mozart-Porträt von Giovanni Antonio Sasso nach Bosio, um 1815
Seite 44/45: „Le Nozze di Figaro", Szenenfoto aus dem Finale des 4. Aktes in
einer Inszenierung von Jean-Pierre Ponnelle bei den Salzburger Festspielen 1987

Idealized portrait of Mozart by Giovanni
Antonio Sasso, based on Bosio, c. 1815
Pages 44/45: "Le Nozze di Figaro,"
photograph of a scene from the finale of
Act IV, in Jean-Pierre Ponnelle's pro-
duction for the Salzburg Festival, 1987

Portrait idéalisé de Mozart par Giovanni
Antonio Sasso d'après Bosio, vers 1815
Pages 44/45 : « Les Noces de Figaro »,
photo du final de l'acte IV dans une mise
en scène de Jean-Pierre Ponnelle au
festival de Salzbourg en 1987

Das Wiener Jahrzehnt

Der Erfolg des „Idomeneo" bedeutet den endgültigen
Bruch mit Salzburg. Mozart überzieht den Urlaub, stürzt
sich ins Münchner Faschingstreiben, macht einen Besuch bei seiner Augsburger Cousine, dem ‚Bäsle', und
folgt nur widerstrebend dem Befehl, Colloredo nachzu-
reisen, um ihm bei dessen Aufenthalt in Wien als Kammermusiker zur Verfügung zu stehen. Mozart begehrt
auf gegen den Dienst, der ihm keine Freiheit läßt, und
fragt sich, „ob ich noch ferners in salzburg meine jungen jahre und mein talent vergraben ... oder warten soll
bis es zu späth ist." Schließlich reicht er noch in Wien
sein Entlassungsgesuch ein, das jedoch von Colloredos
Kammerherrn, Graf Arco, zurückgewiesen wird. Nach
wiederholten Eingaben kommt es zu einem letzten Wort-
gefecht, bei dem Arco ihn mit einem „tritt im arsch" zur
Tür hinausbefördert.

„Ich versichere Sie, daß hier ein Herrlicher ort ist –
und für mein Metier der beste ort von der Welt", schreibt
Mozart aus Wien an seinen Vater, doch der verargt es
ihm, daß er den Hinauswurf riskiert, ja provoziert hat.
Die Entfremdung zwischen ihnen nimmt noch zu, als
Mozart sich mit Konstanze Weber verlobt, der jüngeren
Schwester jener Sängerin, in die er sich in Mannheim
verliebt hatte. Leopold kommt nicht zur Hochzeit, und
auch der Sohn kehrt nur noch einmal nach Salzburg
zurück, um in St. Peter, einer Abteikirche, die nicht dem
Fürsterzbischof untersteht, seine grandiose, doch niemals komplett fertiggestellte C-Moll-Messe aufzuführen
(KV 427, es fehlen Teile des Credo und das Agnus Dei),
wobei Konstanze eine der beiden Sopran-Solostimmen
singt. Bei seinem Gegenbesuch jedoch, anderthalb Jahre
später, kann Leopold Mozart sich davon überzeugen,
daß die Entscheidung seines Sohnes richtig war, denn er
scheint in Geld zu schwimmen, genießt das Wohlwollen
des Kaisers und die Bewunderung Joseph Haydns, des
bedeutendsten Komponisten seiner Zeit: „Ich sage ihnen
vor gott, als ein ehrlicher Mann, ihr sohn ist der größte
Componist, den ich von Person und den Nahmen nach
kenne: er hat geschmack, und über das die größte
Compositionswissenschaft."

Nach Berechungen von Otto Jahn, der zwischen
1856 und 1859 die erste große Mozart-Biographie ver-

The Vienna Decade

The success of "Idomeneo" signified the final break with Salzburg. Mozart overstepped his leave, throwing himself into the Carnival activities and paying a visit to "Bäsle," his cousin in Augsburg. Only with reluctance did he obey Colloredo's summons to follow him to Vienna and place himself at the count's disposal as chamber musician. Mozart chafed against the servitude that allowed him no time to himself, and asked himself "whether I should still continue to bury my youthful years and my talent in Salzburg ... or wait until it's too late." Once in Vienna he finally submitted his letter of resignation, only to have it rejected by Count Arco, Colloredo's chamberlain. After repeated attempts to withdraw from service, it finally came to a battle of words between the musician and the court official in which Arco, according to Mozart, "kicked my ass" out the door.

"I assure you that this is a glorious place—and as my métier, the best in the world," the young man assured his father from Vienna. But it vexed the old man that his son had risked—indeed, provoked—being thrown out. The estrangement increased when Mozart became engaged to Constanze Weber, the younger sister of the singer with whom he had fallen in love in Mannheim. Leopold did not attend the wedding, and the son returned only once more to Salzburg for the performance of his grandiose, but never completed, Mass in C-Minor (K 427; it lacks parts of the "Credo" and the "Agnus Dei"). The Mass was presented in the abbey of St. Peter, which lay outside the jurisdiction of the prince-archbishop, with Constanze singing one of the two solo soprano parts. When Leopold returned the couple's visit eighteen months later, however, he was able to convince himself that his son had made the right choice, for the young Mozart seemed to be swimming in money, and enjoyed both the favor of the emperor and the admiration of Joseph Haydn, the most distinguished of the day: "As a man of honor, I tell you before God that your son is the greatest composer that I know in person or by reputation: He possesses good taste, and beyond that, the greatest understanding of composition."

In the year 1783 alone (according to the estimates of Otto Jahn, who published the first great Mozart bio-

La décennie viennoise

Le succès d'« Idoménée » consomme la rupture définitive avec Salzbourg. Mozart outrepasse son temps de congé, se jette dans les festivités du carnaval de Munich, fait une visite à sa cousine d'Augsbourg, la « Bäsle », et ne suit qu'à contrecœur l'ordre de partir rejoindre Colloredo à Vienne, où il doit se tenir à sa disposition. Révolté contre ce service qui ne lui laisse aucune liberté, Mozart se demande « s'[il va] continuer encore longtemps d'enterrer [ses] jeunes années et [son] talent à Salzbourg [...] ou attendre qu'il soit trop tard. » De Vienne, il finit par remettre sa démission que refuse cependant le chambellan de Colloredo, le comte d'Arco. A la suite de demandes réitérées, ils en arrivent à une dernière joute oratoire au terme de laquelle d'Arco le flanque à la porte « avec un coup de pied au cul ».

« Je vous assure que je me trouve dans un endroit magnifique, et pour mon métier le meilleur endroit au monde », écrit Mozart à son père de Vienne, mais celui-ci lui en veut d'avoir provoqué son renvoi. Le froid entre les deux hommes s'accentue encore quand Mozart se fiance à Constance Weber, la sœur cadette de cette cantatrice dont il s'était épris à Mannheim. Léopold ne vient pas au mariage, et le fils pour sa part ne retourne qu'une fois à Salzbourg, dans le but de faire jouer à Saint-Pierre, une église abbatiale qui ne dépend pas du prince-archevêque, sa grandiose quoique restée toujours inachevée Messe en ut mineur (K. 427), dans laquelle Constance tient l'une des deux parties de soprano. Et pourtant, lorsqu'un an et demi plus tard, Léopold Mozart lui rend sa visite, il peut se rendre compte de ses propres yeux que la décision de son fils était la bonne. Celui-ci semble en effet rouler sur l'or, il jouit de la bienveillance de l'empereur et de l'admiration de Joseph Haydn, le compositeur le plus important de son époque : « Je vous déclare devant Dieu, en honnête homme, que je tiens votre fils pour le plus grand compositeur que je connaisse, tant personnellement que de nom. Il a du goût et en outre, la plus grande science de la composition. »

D'après les calculs d'Otto Jahn, qui entre 1856 et 1859 a publié la première grande biographie de Mozart, le compositeur disposerait, dans la seule année 1783, d'un revenu d'à peu près 2000 florins, et même sans

öffentlichte, verfügt Mozart allein im Jahr 1783 über ein Einkommen von rund 2000 Gulden, wahrscheinlich sogar mehr, auf jeden Fall aber ein Mehrfaches des Organistenlohns in Salzburg. Die Haupteinnahmequelle sind Konzerte, in denen er sich dem Wiener Publikum als Komponist und Pianist empfiehlt. Klavierschüler strömen ihm zu, die Verlagshonorare mehren sich, und auch der Kaiser zeigt sich mit Geldgeschenken erkenntlich, wann immer Mozart vor ihm musiziert. Doch sein aufwendiger Lebensstil – teures Mobiliar, ein Reitpferd, eine Kutsche, elegante Kleidung und auch die kostspielige Leidenschaft für das Billardspiel – zehren den Wohlstand schnell wieder auf.

Als Veranstalter eigener Akademien hat er drei Jahre lang Erfolg, danach schwindet das Interesse an seinen Klavierkonzerten und Mozart beendet den Balanceakt zwischen Konvention und künstlerischer Selbstbehauptung, um sich wieder der Oper zuzuwenden.

Etwa die Hälfte seiner insgesamt 18 Bühnenwerke – die Ballettmusiken und unvollendeten Werke nicht eingerechnet – hat Mozart vor seinem 20. Lebensjahr komponiert. In den Spielplänen unserer Zeit ist freilich nur das letzte Drittel seines Opernschaffens präsent. Auch der 1780 auf der Grenze zwischen Früh- und Reifezeit entstandene „Idomeneo" führt eine Schattenexistenz im Repertoire, ebenso wie „La clemenza di Tito" (KV 621), die Prager Krönungsoper aus dem Todesjahr 1791. Zwischen diesen Werken in ‚seria'-Manier stehen die drei Opern auf Libretti von Lorenzo Da Ponte, umrahmt von der „Entführung aus dem Serail" (KV 384) und der „Zauberflöte" (KV 620), die die Welt der Oper förmlich aus den Angeln heben. Doch so radikal, wie es scheint, bricht Mozart nicht mit der Vergangenheit. Was er anstrebt, ist eher eine Synthese der Gattungstraditionen. Die drei Da-Ponte-Opern spielen virtuos mit ur-italienischen Grundmustern der musikalischen Komödie und, zumal in „Don Giovanni", mit der Vermischung von ‚seria'- und ‚buffa'-Elementen, während die „Entführung" italienische Buffa- und Einflüsse der französischen Opéra comique vereint; ein ‚deutsches' Singspiel ist die „Entführung" nur durch ihre gesprochenen Dialoge. In der „Zauberflöte" hingegen, angesiedelt zwischen Wiener Vorstadtkomödie und großer Oper, ist weniger Verschmelzung als Kontrast das Mittel, die auch dramaturgisch uneinheitliche Konzeption des Werkes umzusetzen.

graphy between 1856 and 1859), Mozart had at his disposal an income of around 2000 gulden—probably even more, but in any case, several times greater than that of an organist in Salzburg. The major portion of his earnings derived from the concerts in which he appeared before the Viennese public in the role of both composer and pianist. In addition, piano students streamed to him, royalties from the publishers were increasing, and even the emperor demonstrated his appreciation with gifts of gold whenever Mozart performed before him. And yet the young man's extravagant lifestyle—expensive furniture, a riding horse, a coach, elegant clothing, as well as his costly passion for billiards—gnawed quickly away at his wealth. He enjoyed three years of success as the promoter and organizer of his own subscription concerts, but then interest in his piano concerts began to wane. Mozart finally ended this balancing act between convention and artistic self-fulfillment in order to devote himself again to the opera.

Before his twentieth year, Mozart had already composed approximately half of his in toto eighteen works for the stage (excluding ballet music and unfinished pieces). In modern-day programs, only the last third of his operatic works are actually performed. Even "Idomeneo," composed in 1780 on the border between his early and mature composition, boasts only a shadowy existence in the Mozart repertoire—a fate shared also by "La clemenza de Tito" (K 621), the Prague coronation opera composed in 1791, the year of Mozart's death. Between these two works stand the three operas based on the librettos by Lorenzo Da Ponte. Composed in the manner of the *opera seria*, and framed by the "Entführung aus den Serail" (K 384, "The Abduction from the Seraglio"), and "Die Zauberflöte" (K 620, "The Magic Flute"), these three works literally changed operatic history. And yet, as radical as his work seemed, Mozart did not break with the past. Rather, what he strove for was a synthesis of traditional genres. All three Da Ponte operas play with the old Italian patterns of musical comedy; "Don Giovanni" in particular draws from a combination of *seria* and *buffa* elements; whereas the "Entführung" unites Italian *buffa* with influences of the French *opéra comique* traditions. The "Entführung" is related to the so-called "German" Singspiel only by virtue of its spoken dialogue. On the other hand, in the "Zauberflöte," standing as it does somewhere between Viennese bourgeois com-

doute plus. Ce sont les concerts, à l'occasion desquels il se présente au public viennois comme compositeur et pianiste, qui constituent sa principale source de revenus. Les élèves affluent à ses leçons de piano, les droits d'auteur se multiplient, et chaque fois qu'il fait de la musique pour lui, l'empereur lui manifeste sa reconnaissance en lui offrant des sommes d'argent. Mais son train de vie dispendieux (des meubles chers, un cheval de course, une calèche, des vêtements élégants ainsi qu'une passion coûteuse pour le billard) a tôt fait de venir à bout de cette prospérité.

L'organisation de ses propres «académies» lui vaut du succès pendant trois ans, au terme desquels l'intérêt pour ses récitals de piano retombe. Mozart met alors un terme à ce numéro d'équilibre entre la convention musicale et l'affirmation artistique de soi pour se tourner de nouveau vers l'opéra.

Sur un total de dix-huit œuvres dramatiques, Mozart en a composé à peu près la moitié, sans compter les musiques de ballet et autres œuvres inachevées, avant sa vingtième année. L'opéra «Idoménée», qui en 1780 occupait une position charnière entre œuvre de jeunesse et maturité, est tenu à l'écart du répertoire tout comme «La clémence de Titus» (K. 621), composé en 1791, l'année de sa mort, pour le couronnement à Prague de Léopold II. Entre ces œuvres qui ressortent du genre de l'«opera seria», il y a les trois opéras composés sur des livrets de Lorenzo Da Ponte, elles-mêmes encadrées par «L'Enlèvement au sérail» (K. 384) et «La Flûte enchantée» (K. 620) qui, d'un point de vue formel, bouleversent l'univers de l'opéra. Et cependant, pour aussi radical qu'il en ait l'air, Mozart ne rompt pas avec le passé. Ce qu'il ambitionne, c'est plutôt de parvenir à une synthèse des genres traditionnels. Les trois opéras de Da Ponte jouent en virtuoses de schémas de la comédie musicale italienne, combinent, en particulier dans «Don Giovanni», des éléments de l'«opera seria» et de l'opéra bouffe, tandis que «L'Enlèvement» mêle au «buffa» italien des influences de l'opéra comique français; si «L'Enlèvement» est un singspiel «allemand», ce n'est pas seulement à cause de ses dialogues parlés. A l'inverse dans «La Flûte enchantée», qui se situe entre la comédie viennoise de faubourg et le grand opéra, c'est moins l'amalgame que le contraste qui est le moyen d'assurer la cohésion d'une œuvre qui en est dépourvue jusque dans sa conception dramaturgique.

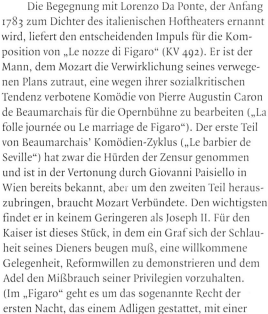

Die Begegnung mit Lorenzo Da Ponte, der Anfang 1783 zum Dichter des italienischen Hoftheaters ernannt wird, liefert den entscheidenden Impuls für die Komposition von „Le nozze di Figaro" (KV 492). Er ist der Mann, dem Mozart die Verwirklichung seines verwegenen Plans zutraut, eine wegen ihrer sozialkritischen Tendenz verbotene Komödie von Pierre Augustin Caron de Beaumarchais für die Opernbühne zu bearbeiten („La folle journée ou Le marriage de Figaro"). Der erste Teil von Beaumarchais' Komödien-Zyklus („Le barbier de Seville") hat zwar die Hürden der Zensur genommen und ist in der Vertonung durch Giovanni Paisiello in Wien bereits bekannt, aber um den zweiten Teil herauszubringen, braucht Mozart Verbündete. Den wichtigsten findet er in keinem Geringeren als Joseph II. Für den Kaiser ist dieses Stück, in dem ein Graf sich der Schlauheit seines Dieners beugen muß, eine willkommene Gelegenheit, Reformwillen zu demonstrieren und dem Adel den Mißbrauch seiner Privilegien vorzuhalten. (Im „Figaro" geht es um das sogenannte Recht der ersten Nacht, das einem Adligen gestattet, mit einer

edy and grand opera, Mozart turned to contrast rather than fusion to realize the divergent dramatical and musical conceptions of the work.

The meeting with Lorenzo Da Ponte, who had been appointed poet to the Italian court theater in early 1783, also provided the decisive impulse for the composition of "Le nozze di Figaro" (K 492, "The Marriage of Figaro"). Mozart entrusted Da Ponte with the execution of his daring plan to rework a comedy by Pierre Augustin Caron de Beaumarchais ("La folle journée ou Le marriage de Figaro"), which had been banned from the stage for its socially critical sentiments. The first part of Beaumarchais' comedy cycle ("Le barbier de Seville") had, however, passed the hurdles of the censor and, set to music by Giovanni Paisiello, it was already familiar to Viennese audiences. In order to produce the second part of the work, Mozart needed allies—the most important of whom he found in no less a figure than the emperor himself. For Joseph II, a play in which a count must bow to the cleverness of his servant provided a welcome opportunity to demonstrate his desire for reform and to

Seite 47 oben: Das Camesina-Haus („Figaro-Haus") in der Großen Schuler-straße. Mozart bewohnt die Beletage mit Erker. Aquarell von Richard Moser, 1905
Seite 47 unten: Heutiges Interieur des „Figaro-Hauses", Mozarts Wohnung von 1784 bis 1787
Rechts: Kostümbilder zu „Figaros Hoch-zeit". Wiener Theaterzeitung, 19. Jahr-hundert

Page 47, top: The Camesina house („Figaro House") on Grosse Schuler-strasse, where Mozart lived on the *belle etage*, in an apartment with an oriel. Watercolor by Richard Moser, 1905
Page 47, bottom: Interior of the „Figaro House" today, where Mozart had an apartment from 1784 to 1787.
Right: Costume drawings from „The Marriage of Figaro." Viennese theater newspaper, 19th century

Page 47, en haut: La Camesina (la «mai-son de Figaro») dans la Große Schuler-straße. Mozart loge au premier étage, là où se trouve l'oriel. Aquarelle de Richard Moser, 1905
Page 47, en bas: L'intérieur actuel de la « maison de Figaro» où Mozart habitera de 1784 à 1787
A droite: Illustrations de costumes des «Noces de Figaro». Wiener Theater-zeitung, 19ᵉ siècle

Costume-Bild zur Theaterzeitung.   No. 63

Eine Scene aus Figaros Hochzeit.

Wien im Bureau der Theaterzeitung, Rauhensteingasse No 926

Seite 48 links: Mozart im Hause Duschek. Das Musikerehepaar Josepha (1753–1824) und Franz Xaver Duschek (1731–1799) ge-hört zu Mozarts engsten Prager Freun-den. In der Villa Bertramka, dem Prager Landsitz der Duscheks, ist Mozart gern zu Gast. Kolorierte Silhouette, anonym, entstanden zum Andenken an die Urauf-führung des „Don Giovanni" (1787)
Seite 48 rechts: Martha Elisabeth Baronin Waldstätten (1744–1811), eine lebenslusti-ge Frau von nicht ganz untadeligem Ruf, gehört zu Mozarts engstem Freundes-kreis während der ersten Wiener Jahre. Silhouette von François Gonard, 1781

Page 48, left: Mozart at the Duschek house. The musical couple Josepha (1753–1824) and Franz Xaver Duschek (1731–1799) were among Mozart's closest friends in Prague. Mozart was often their guest at the Villa Bertramka, their country estate near Prague. Anonymous colored silhou-ette, made as a souvenir for the premier of „Don Giovanni" (1787).
Page 48, right: Martha Elisabeth, Baroness Waldstätten (1744–1811), a spirited, fun-loving woman of not entirely unblemished reputation, was a member of Mozart's inner circle of friends during his years in Vienna. Silhouette by F. Gonard, 1781

Page 48, à gauche: Martha Elisabeth chez les Du-schek. Le couple de musiciens Josepha et Franz Xaver Duschek fait partie du cercle d'intimes de Mozart à Prague. Mozart aime séjourner à la Villa Bertramka, pro-priété des Duschek à Prague. Silhouette anonyme, réalisée en souvenir de la pre-mière de «Don Giovanni» (1787)
Page 48, à droite: Martha Elisabeth, baronne Waldstätten (1744–1811), une femme aimant la vie, pas très respectable au demeurant, est l'une des meilleures amies de Mozart pendant ses premières années à Vienne. Silhouette de François Gonard, 1781

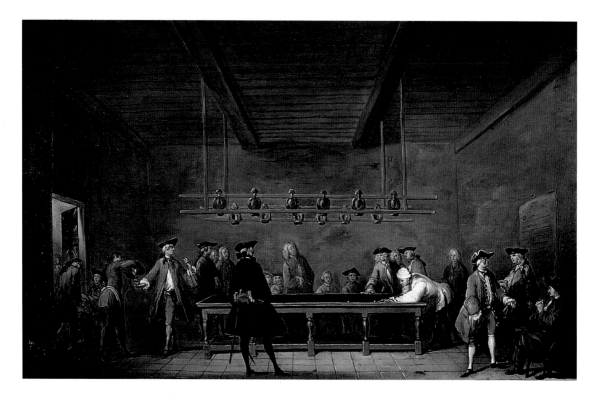

La rencontre avec Lorenzo Da Ponte, qui est nommé début 1783 poète du théâtre italien de la cour, donnera une impulsion décisive à la composition des « Noces de Figaro » (K. 492). Da Ponte est l'homme auquel Mozart confie la réalisation de son audacieux projet de transposer pour l'opéra une comédie de Pierre Augustin Caron de Beaumarchais, « La folle journée ou le mariage de Figaro », interdite pour ses tendances critiques envers la société. Il est vrai que la première partie du cycle de comédies de Beaumarchais, « Le Barbier de Séville », a su déjouer les pièges de la censure et que sa mise en musique par Giovanni Paisiello l'a déjà fait connaître à Vienne. Mais pour en monter la seconde partie, Mozart aura besoin d'alliés, dont le plus important ne sera personne d'autre que Joseph II lui-même. Cette pièce dans laquelle un comte est obligé de s'incliner devant la débrouillardise de son valet est pour l'empereur une bonne occasion de manifester sa volonté d'entreprendre des réformes et de reprocher à la noblesse le mauvais usage qu'elle fait de ses privilèges.

„Die Billardpartie", eines der Hauptvergnügen Mozarts in Wien. Gemälde von Jean-Baptiste Simeon, 18. Jahrhundert. Für die Wohnung im Camesina-Haus, in der es auch ein Billardzimmer gibt, zahlt Mozart 460 Gulden jährlich.

"The Game of Billiards" was one of Mozart's chief pleasures in Vienna. Painting by Jean-Baptiste Simeon, 18th century. For the apartment in the Camesina House, in which there was also a billiard room, Mozart paid an annual rent of 460 gulden.

« La Partie de billard », l'un des plus grands plaisirs de Mozart à Vienne. Tableau de Jean-Baptiste Simeon, 18ᵉ siècle. Le loyer de l'appartement de la maison Camesina, qui abrite aussi une salle de billard, s'élève à 460 florins par an.

Dienerin, wenn sie sich verheiratet, das Hochzeitsbett zu teilen.)

Mozarts ungeheuer temporeiche Komödie, die nicht nur den Keim der Revolution in sich birgt, sondern auch den vertrauten Schematismus der italienischen Buffo-Oper weit hinter sich läßt, stößt beim adligen Publikum des Wiener Hoftheaters auf begreifliche Zurückhaltung. In Prag allerdings, wo sie noch im selben Jahr, 1786, nachgespielt wird, hat sie den gegenteiligen Effekt: Die Adelskritik wird sogar von der Aristokratie bejubelt, und auch die musikalisch revolutionäre Verflechtung von Rezitativ und Arie mit quirligen Ensembleszenen entfacht beim musikkundigen Publikum wahre Stürme der Begeisterung. Von seinen böhmischen Verehrern eingeladen, kann Mozart die Wonnen des Figaro-Fiebers, das die ganze Stadt erfaßt hat, miterleben: „hier wird von nichts gesprochen als vom – figaro; nichts gespielt, geblasen und gepfiffen als – figaro: keine opera besucht als – figaro und Ewig figaro; gewis grosse Ehre für mich". Den Auftrag für eine weitere Oper, „Don Giovanni" (KV 527), die in der nächsten Wintersaison am Prager Nationaltheater Premiere haben soll, bringt er mit nach Wien zurück.

Am 28. Mai 1787, während der Arbeit an dem neuen Werk, die ihn stark beansprucht, stirbt sein Vater. Mozart reist nicht zur Beerdigung, um die Versteigerung des Nachlasses kümmert sich seine Schwester. Es bedarf keiner Tiefenpsychologie, um zu erkennen, daß der Verlust des Vaters die Todesschatten in „Don Giovanni" – nicht nur in der gespenstischen Friedhofsszene – noch düsterer gemacht hat, als es der ursprünglichen Konzeption dieses ‚dramma giocoso' entsprach. Die Geschichte eines Wüstlings, der seiner gerechten Strafe nicht entgeht, ist ein makabrer Spaß, aber auch eine Offenbarung der menschlichen Seele, denn Mozart stellt in diesem ‚heiteren Drama' nicht nur den Bösewicht als einen Getriebenen bloß, sondern entlarvt auch die Tugendsamen, die ihn verurteilen.

Eine vielleicht noch größere Kunst der Charakterzeichnung zeigt „Così fan tutte" (KV 588), äußerlich eine Typen- und Verwechslungskomödie neapolitanischen Zuschnitts, doch in der subtilen Verschränkung von Gefühls- und Handlungsebene fast ein Kammerspiel im Sinne des modernen, bürgerlichen Theaters. Den hochdotierten Auftrag zu dieser Oper erhielt Mozart wahrscheinlich direkt vom Kaiser, der jedoch im Februar

Antonio Salieri (1750–1825), Kammerkompositeur, Kapellmeister der italienischen Oper und seit 1788 Hofkapellmeister, ist eine der erfolg- und einflußreichsten Musikerpersönlichkeiten in Wien. Zeitgenössisches Porträt von unbekannter Hand

Antonio Salieri (1750–1825), chamber composer, *Kapellmeister* of the Italian Opera in Vienna and court *Kapellmeister* since 1788, was one of the most successful and influential musical personalities in Vienna. Contemporary portrait by an unknown artist

Antonio Salieri (1750–1825), compositeur italien, maître de chapelle de l'opéra italien et, à partir de 1788, maître de chapelle impérial, est l'un des musiciens ayant le plus de succès et le plus d'influence à Vienne. Portrait d'époque par un peintre anonyme

flout the nobility for its misuse of privilege. ("Figaro" revolves around the so-called "droit du seigneur," which granted a nobleman the right to sleep with a vassal's bride on the wedding night.)

Mozart's extremely lively and fast-paced comedy, which not only harbors the seed of revolution but also leaves the trusted schematic of the Italian *opera buffa* far behind, understandably met with reservation on the part of the noble audience of the Viennese court theater. When the opera was mounted later that same year (1786) in Prague, however, it called forth the opposite response: The aristocracy even celebrated the criticism leveled against itself, and the musically revolutionary interweaving of recitative and aria with bustling ensemble scenes also sparked a storm of enthusiasm among the musically knowledgeable public. Invited by his Bohemian admirers, Mozart was able to share in the ecstasy of the Figaro fever that held the whole city in its grasp: "Here no one speaks of anything but—Figaro; nothing is played, blown, or whistled but—Figaro; no opera attended but—Figaro, and always Figaro; certainly a great honor to me." He returned from Vienna with the commission for another opera, "Don Giovanni" (K 527), that was to have its premier at the National Theater of Prague in the next winter season.

On May 28, 1787, while the composer was hard at work on the new opera which placed heavy demands on him, Leopold Mozart died. The son did not travel to the funeral, and his sister handled the auctioning of the estate. It requires no depth psychology to recognize that the loss of his father deepened the shadow of death hovering over "Don Giovanni"—and not only in the eerie cemetery scene—beyond what corresponded to the original comic conception of the *dramma giocoso*. The tale of a libertine who meets up with his just punishment is a macabre kind of comedy, but also a revelation of the human soul, for in his "amusing drama," Mozart not only reveals the villain as a driven soul, but also unmasks the virtuous who condemn him.

A possibly even greater skill in the depiction of character is evident in "Così fan tutte" (K 588). Ostensibly a comedy of type and mistaken identity in the Neapolitan tradition, its subtle interlacing of various levels of feeling and plot make it almost into a chamber play in the sense of modern, bourgeois theater. Mozart was well-paid for the opera, probably receiving his commis-

Cette comédie aux multiples rebondissements, qui ne se contente pas de contenir en elle un ferment de révolution, mais a des relents d'opéra bouffe italien dont on retrouve des schémas familiers, se heurte auprès du public noble du théâtre impérial de Vienne à la réserve qu'on peut imaginer. A Prague en revanche, où elle est reprise cette même année 1786, elle produit un effet contraire. La critique de la noblesse est saluée par l'aristocratie elle-même, et l'imbrication, tout à fait révolutionnaire du point de vue musical, de récitatifs et d'arias dans des scènes d'ensemble très animées soulève des tonnes d'applaudissements parmi le public connaisseur. Invité par ses admirateurs de Bohême, Mozart peut alors goûter les délices de la « figaromania » qui s'est emparée de toute la ville : « on ne parle ici de rien d'autre que de... Figaro ; on ne joue, sur un vent ou un autre instrument, et ne siffle que... Figaro ; on ne voit d'autre opéra que... Figaro et toujours Figaro ; un grand honneur pour moi en réalité ». De retour à Vienne, il rapporte dans ses bagages la commande d'un nouvel opéra, « Don Giovanni » (K. 527), dont la création doit avoir lieu en hiver, dans le cadre de la prochaine saison du théâtre national de Prague.

Le 28 mai 1787, alors qu'il travaille à cette nouvelle œuvre qui l'accapare fortement, son père décède. Mozart ne se rend pas à l'enterrement, et c'est sa sœur qui s'occupe de vendre la succession aux enchères. Point n'est besoin d'être psychologue des profondeurs pour se rendre compte que la perte du père a rendu les ombres de la mort de « Don Giovanni » plus sinistres encore qu'elles ne l'étaient dans la conception originale de ce « dramma giocoso ». L'histoire d'un débauché qui n'échappe pas à un châtiment légitime est peut-être une farce macabre, mais aussi une révélation de l'âme humaine dans la mesure où Mozart ne se contente pas de ridiculiser le méchant en faisant s'ouvrir le sol sous lui, mais dénonce les âmes vertueuses qui le condamnent.

L'art de peindre les caractères est peut-être encore plus évident dans « Così fan tutte » (K. 588). Si on a affaire en apparence à une comédie de caractères traversée de quiproquos dans le style napolitain, l'enchevêtrement du sentiment et de l'action fait qu'on se trouve en réalité presque en présence d'un « kammerspiel » au sens moderne du théâtre bourgeois. Mozart a vraisemblablement reçu cette commande de l'empereur lui-même, qui décédera en février 1790, quelques semaines après la création, sans avoir vu une seule des cinq représentations

Der Maler Max Slevogt ließ sich von dem berühmten Don-Giovanni-Darsteller Francisco d'Andrade zu mehreren Bildern inspirieren; „Die Champagner-Arie" entstand 1902.
Seite 53: Mozart-Porträt (Wachsrelief) von Leonhard Posch, um 1789

The painter Max Slevogt was inspired by Francisco d'Andrade, famous for his role as Don Giovanni, to paint several pictures; the *Champagne Aria* was done in 1902.
Page 53: Portrait of Mozart (wax relief) by Leonhard Posch, c. 1789

Le célèbre interprète de Don Giovanni, Francisco d'Andrade, a inspiré plusieurs tableaux au peintre Max Slevogt; « L'Air du champagne » a été réalisé en 1902.
Page 53: Portrait de Mozart (relief sur cire) de Leonhard Posch, vers 1789

Das Theater an der Wien, Uraufführungsort von Beethovens „Fidelio" und Nachfolgebau des Freihaustheaters auf der Wieden, in dem „Die Zauberflöte" Premiere hat. Kolorierte Radierung, um 1820. Mit dem Neubau des Theaters an der Wien, des damals größten Theaters in der Stadt, geht ein Lebenstraum Emanuel Schikaneders in Erfüllung. Der Theaterunternehmer und Schauspieler ist nicht nur der Textdichter der „Zauberflöte", sondern auch der erste Darsteller des Papageno. Auf dem Höhepunkt seines Ruhms ist er Besitzer einer prachtvollen Villa, des sogenannten Schikanederschlößls, in dem er einen Saal mit Motiven der „Zauberflöte" ausgestalten läßt.

The Theater an der Wien, where Beethoven's "Fidelio" premiered, and the subsequently built Freihaustheater auf der Weiden, where "Die Zauberflöte" was first performed. Colored etching, c. 1820. The rebuilding of the Theater an der Wien, at that time the largest theater in the city, meant the fulfillment of a dream of Emanuel Schikaneder. The theater businessman and actor was not only the poet of the "Zauberflöte," but also first Papageno. At the height of this fame, he owned a luxurious villa, known as the "Schikanederschlössl" (the little Schikaneder castle), in which he had a room decorated with motifs from the "Zauberflöte."

Le théâtre «an der Wien», où se déroula la première du «Fidelio» de Beethoven est construit à l'emplacement du théâtre «auf der Wieden» où a lieu la première de «La Flûte enchantée». Gravure coloriée, vers 1820. Avec ce nouveau théâtre, à l'époque le plus grand de la ville, le rêve d'Emanuel Schikaneder est exaucé. Cet entrepreneur de théâtre et comédien n'a pas seulement écrit les textes de «La Flûte enchantée», il est aussi le premier à incarner Papageno. A l'apogée de sa célébrité il sera le propriétaire d'une splendide villa, le Schikanederschlößl (le petit palais de Schikaneder); il fera décorer une salle avec des motifs de «La Flûte enchantée».

1790, wenige Wochen nach der Premiere, stirbt, ohne eine der fünf Aufführungen im Burgtheater gesehen zu haben. Infolge der Staatstrauer wird „Così" erst im Juni wiederaufgenommen und noch fünfmal gespielt, danach zu Mozarts Lebzeiten nicht mehr.

Von den in Wien entstandenen Beiträgen zur Orchester- und Kammermusik gelten etliche als krönende Beispiele ihrer jeweiligen Gattung, seien es die als Verneigung vor dem großen Kollegen Joseph Haydn entstandenen Streichquartette, die Hornkonzerte, die Klaviersonaten oder auch Arbeiten wie „Eine kleine Nachtmusik" (KV 525) und die Bläser-Serenade in B-Dur („Gran Partita", KV 361). Doch keine Werkgruppe nimmt eine so überragende Stellung ein wie die drei letzten Sinfonien in Es-Dur (KV 543), G-Moll (KV 550) und C-Dur (KV 551), geschrieben im Sommer 1790 in einem Zeitraum von knapp zwei Monaten. Es ist nicht erwiesen, daß Mozart sie auch nur ein einziges Mal gehört hat, denn möglicherweise kam das Konzert, für das sie bestimmt waren, nicht zustande.

Fast vierzig seiner insgesamt mehr als fünfzig Sinfonien sind Jugendwerke, in denen die Erfahrungen seiner Reisen und das Talent, „alle art und styl vom Compositions annehmen und nachahmen" zu können, ihren Niederschlag gefunden haben. Nur selten jedoch – etwa in der ‚kleinen' G-Moll-Sinfonie (KV 183) und der Sinfonie in A-Dur (KV 201) – ist Mozart mit den Möglichkeiten der Gattung in ähnlich experimenteller Weise verfahren wie Joseph Haydn. Der Höhe seiner Kunst nähert Mozart sich erst Anfang der achtziger Jahre an („Linzer"-Sinfonie in C-Dur, KV 425), auf dem Gebiet des Streichquartetts noch später. Auch die für Prag geschriebene D-Dur-Sinfonie (KV 504), deren dramatischer Gestus die Nähe zu „Figaro" und „Don Giovanni" verrät, und die erste der drei letzten Sinfonien bleiben äußerlich dem Vorbild Haydnscher Sinfonien verhaftet (Adagio-Einleitung), in der thematischen Arbeit jedoch geht Mozart eigene Wege und stößt dabei in ganz andere Dimensionen vor.

Das zunächst unspektakulär, fast beiläufig erscheinende Hauptthema der G-Moll-Sinfonie entfaltet sich mit federnder Energie in immer neuen motivischen Absplitterungen, die auch die leidenschaftlich erregte Durchführung beherrschen. Dem ausladenden zweiten Satz mit weitgespannten Melodiebögen über einem eigenartig stockenden Grundrhythmus folgt ein fast

sion directly from the emperor, who, however, died in February 1790, a few weeks after the premier, without having attended any of the five performances in the Burgtheater. Official state mourning prevented the staging of "Così" until June, when it was once again performed five times—and then never again during Mozart's lifetime.

Among Mozart's contributions to orchestral and chamber music composed during his decade in Vienna, many works stand as crowning examples of their given genres, such as the string quartets composed in homage to his great colleague Joseph Haydn, the horn concertos, the piano sonatas, or even works like "Eine kleine Nachtmusik" (K 525), and the Wind Serenade in B Major (K 361, "Gran Partita"). But no group of works achieves a rank more eminent than that of the three last symphonies in E-flat Major (K 543s), G Minor (K 550), and C Major (K551), composed within barely two months of each other in the summer of 1790. There is no indication that Mozart ever heard these works performed, for it seems possible that the concert for which they were composed never in fact took place.

Almost forty of Mozart's more than fifty symphonies are works of his youth reflecting both his travel experiences and his talent for "assimilating and imitating all kinds and styles of composition." Only rarely, for example in the "little" Symphony in G Minor (K 183) or the Symphony in A Major (K 201), did Mozart treat the possibilities of the genre in a similarly experimental manner as Joseph Haydn. Mozart reached the height of his powers only at the beginning of the 1780s with the "Linzer" Symphony in C Major (K 425); in the genre of string quartet the zenith came even later. In its dramatic gestic, the Symphony in D Major (K 504), written for Prague, discloses its proximity to "Figaro" and "Don Giovanni." Both this work and the first of the final three symphonies remain superficially bound to the model of the Haydn symphony (Adagio introduction); but thematically Mozart was pursuing his own paths, and in fact was moving in an entirely different direction.

The main theme of the Symphony in G Minor at first appears unspectacular, almost incidental, but it splinters with elastic energy into ever new motives that also control the passionately stirring development. After the sweeping second movement with its broad melodic arches constructed over a uniquely hesitating basic

Aufnahmezeremonie in einer Wiener Loge. Gemälde von Ignaz Unterberger, um 1784. Mozart ist seit 1784 Freimaurer und führt ein Jahr später auch seinen Vater in die Loge ein. Das Freimaurertum ist in bürgerlichen und adligen Kreisen Wiens weit verbreitet; viele von Mozarts Freunden, unter ihnen Joseph Haydn, sind Logenmitglieder. Mozart hat verschiedentlich für freimaurerische Anlässe komponiert, auch „Die Zauberflöte" macht zahlreiche Anleihen bei Ritualen und Symbolen der Freimaurerei.

Initiation ceremony into a Viennese Masonic lodge. Painting by Ignaz Unterberger, c. 1784. Mozart had become a Freemason in 1784 and one year later introduced his father to the lodge. Freemasonry was widespread in the bourgeois and noble circles of Vienna: Many of Mozart's friends, including Joseph Haydn, were lodge memebers. Mozart had at various times composed for Masonic occasions, and »Die Zauberflöte« also borrowed much from the rituals and symbols of the Freemasons.

Cérémonie d'admission dans une loge viennoise. Tableau d'Ignaz Unterberger, vers 1784. Mozart est franc-maçon depuis 1784 et, un an plus tard, il introduit aussi son père dans la loge. La franc-maçonnerie est très répandue dans les cercles bourgeois et aristocratiques viennois; de nombreux amis de Mozart, entre autres Joseph Haydn, sont eux aussi maçons. Mozart a composé à diverses reprises pour des fêtes franc-maçonniques. De nombreux motifs de «La Flûte enchantée» sont empruntés aux rituels et symboles de la franc-maçonnerie.

du Burgtheater. En raison du deuil national, « Così » ne sera repris qu'en juin. L'opéra sera joué encore cinq fois, les dernières du vivant de Mozart.

Parmi les contributions à la musique symphonique et à la musique de chambre qu'il a écrites à Vienne, quelques-unes sont considérées comme des exemples qui portent au plus haut degré de perfection leur genre respectif, que ce soient les quatuors à cordes, composés en hommage au grand confrère Joseph Haydn, les concertos pour cor, les sonates pour piano ou encore des travaux comme « Une petite musique de nuit » (K. 525) ou la Sérénade pour vents en si bémol majeur (« Gran Partita », K. 361). Mais aucun ensemble d'œuvres n'occupe une place d'une envergure comparable à celle des trois dernières symphonies en mi bémol majeur (K. 543), sol mineur (K. 550) et ut majeur (K. 551), écrites pendant l'été 1790 sur une période de tout juste deux mois.

Sur un total de plus de cinquante symphonies, presque quarante sont des œuvres de jeunesse dans lesquelles se sont manifestés l'expérience de ses voyages ainsi que son talent à « assimiler et à reproduire toutes les formes et tous les styles de composition ». Mozart n'a pourtant que rarement, si ce n'est peut-être dans la « petite » symphonie en sol mineur (K. 183) et la symphonie en la majeur (K. 201), exploité les possibilités du genre avec autant de hardiesse que Joseph Haydn. Ce n'est qu'au début des années quatre-vingt que Mozart approche du sommet de son art (Symphonie « Linz » en ut majeur, K. 425), plus tard encore en ce qui concerne le domaine du quatuor à cordes. Si la symphonie « Prague » en ré majeur (K. 504), dont l'atmosphère dramatique est très proche de « Figaro » et de « Don Giovanni », et la première des trois dernières symphonies restent en apparence attachées au modèle haydnien (l'adagio introductif), Mozart emprunte cependant dans le travail thématique des voies qui lui sont propres et explore ainsi de tout autres dimensions.

Le thème principal de la symphonie en sol mineur, qui de prime abord semble peu brillant et même presque secondaire, s'épanouit avec énergie et souplesse à travers un renouvellement constant et une fulgurance de motifs qui se retrouvent également au niveau de l'exécution, tout entière gouvernée par la passion. Au second mouvement plus apaisé, dans lequel d'amples lignes mélodiques se déploient sur un rythme de base singulièrement hésitant, succède un menuet presque brutal qui

Theaterzettel der Uraufführung von „Così fan tutte" in Wien am 26. Januar 1790. In den deutschen Fassungen dieser Komödie der Verführung ist von den deutlichen sexuellen Anspielungen des Textdichters Da Ponte nicht viel übriggeblieben. Diese Verharmlosung macht aus dem Stück einen neckischen Mummenschanz, der mit der Gefühlswelt junger, in ihrer Liebe zutiefst verunsicherter Menschen kaum noch etwas zu tun hat.

Theater bill for the premier of "Così fan tutte" in Vienna, January 26, 1790. The German version of the libretto by Da Ponte virtually does away with the sexual innuendos of this seduction comedy. This whitewashing makes the opera into a coquettish masquerade, far removed from the realm of feeling inhabited by the the young lovers thrown into the deepest uncertainty by their love.

Bulletin théâtral de la première de « Così fan tutte » à Vienne, le 26 janvier 1790. Dans les versions allemandes de cette comédie de la séduction, il ne reste pas grand-chose des allusions sexuelles non déguisées de leur auteur, Da Ponte. Ainsi édulcorée, la pièce devient une mascarade taquine bien éloignée des sentiments de jeunes gens dont les certitudes amoureuses sont fortement ébranlées.

ruppiges, auf beethovensche Scherzi vorausweisendes Menuett, dessen thematisches Material im Finale dann einer wahren Zerreißprobe unterzogen wird. Diese thematische Verklammerung der Sätze erreicht ihren Höhepunkt in der letzten Sinfonie, der man schon bald nach Mozarts Tod den Namen eines Gottes, „Jupiter", beigelegt hat, als Ausdruck grenzenloser Bewunderung für die darin waltende kreative Kraft und Ordnung. Alle Sätze mit Ausnahme des zweiten greifen auf die thematische Substanz des Hauptsatzes zurück. Die kontrastierenden Themenglieder differenzieren sich im Finale nochmals aus und verschmelzen schließlich, fugenartig aufgetürmt, in einer beispiellosen Synthese von Sonatenprinzip und strenger Satztechnik, die auch Haydn und alle nachfolgenden Komponistengenerationen tief beeindruckt hat.

Die Tatsache, daß Mozart – nach sechs Umzügen seit 1782 – zwischen Dezember 1787 und Anfang 1789 dreimal die Wohnung wechselt, läßt sich als Zeichen finanzieller Bedrängnis deuten. Im Juni 1788, während der Arbeit an den drei letzten Sinfonien und wenige Monate nach der Geburt seines vierten Kindes (das wie schon das erste und dritte noch im ersten Lebensjahr stirbt) geht er seinen Freund und Logenbruder Michael Puchberg um ein längerfristiges Darlehen an, weitere Bettelbriefe folgen. Die Summe der kleineren und größeren Beträge, mit denen Puchberg ihm in den nächsten Jahren aushilft, beläuft sich auf über 1400 Gulden. Dagegen stehen an festen Einnahmen nur 800 Gulden jährlich, die Mozart seit 1787 als „k.k. Hof-Musik-Compositor" empfängt, ein Salär, an das sich allein die Verpflichtung knüpft, Tänze für die Maskenbälle am Wiener Hof zu liefern.

Nach dem Tod des Kaisers und der Ernennung seines Nachfolgers Leopold II. dreht sich die Schuldenspirale immer schneller. Mozart bleibt Hofkomponist, erhält aber keine weiteren Aufträge. Während seine Frau versucht, die angespannte Finanzlage durch eine Umschuldung in den Griff zu bekommen, reist er zur Kaiserkrönung nach Frankfurt, einem Ereignis, das zigtausend Besucher anlockt. Doch weil er nicht zum Troß der 15 Kammermusiker gehört, die Leopold II. begleiten, muß er „Silberzeug" versetzen, um die Fahrt zu finanzieren. Die Rechnung geht nicht auf. Das einzige Konzert, das in Frankfurt zustandekommt, verläuft „von Seiten der Ehre herrlich, aber in Betreff des Geldes mager".

rhythm, there follows an almost abrupt minuet, predictive of Beethoven's scherzi, whose thematic material then undergoes a truly grueling test of endurance in the finale. This thematic intertwining of the movements reaches its apotheosis in the last symphony, which soon after Mozart's death was dubbed the "Jupiter", a title whose reference to divinity was as an expression of boundless admiration for the creative force and order that govern it. All movements except the second draw from the thematic substance of the principal theme. The contrasting thematic elements distinguish themselves once more in the finale, only to merge together in the end, towering upon one another in fugue-like fashion in an unprecedented synthesis of the sonata principle and rigorous compositional technique that deeply impressed not only Haydn but all subsequent generations of composers.

The fact that Mozart, after having moving six times since 1782, changed his quarters again three times between December 1787 and the beginning of 1789 must be taken as a sign of his financial difficulties. In June 1788, while working on the last three symphonies and awaiting the birth of his fourth child (which like the first and third was to die within its first year), Mozart approached his friend and lodge brother Michael Puchberg for a long-term loan; other letters of entreaty followed. The total of the smaller and larger sums lent by Puchberg during the subsequent years amounted to more than 1,400 gulden, in contrast to Mozart's regular annual income of only 800 gulden, which he had been receiving since 1787 as "composer of royal and imperial courtmusic"—a salary tied to the single duty of providing dance music for the masked balls at the Viennese court.

After the emperor's death and the designation of Leopold II as his successor, Mozart fell with increasing speed into a spiral of debt. He remained court composer, but received no further commissions. While his wife attempted to deal with the strained financial situation by restructuring the debt, Mozart set off for the imperial coronation in Frankfurt, drawn like many thousands of others to the great event. Because he was not a member of the retinue of fifteen chamber musicians accompanying Leopold, he had to pawn silverware to finance the trip. But matters did not work out as he hoped. His only concert in Frankfurt, he reported, came off "gloriously from the standpoint of honor, but meager as far as money is concerned."

annonce les scherzos de Beethoven et dont le matériau
thématique se trouve véritablement malmené dans le
final. Cet enchevêtrement thématique des phrases musicales culmine dans la dernière symphonie, à laquelle on
a donné, peu de temps seulement après la mort de Mozart, le nom d'un dieu, «Jupiter», en signe d'admiration
inconditionnelle pour la force créatrice et l'harmonie
qu'on y sent à l'œuvre. Tous les mouvements à l'excep-
tion du second reprennent la substance thématique du
motif principal. On retrouve dans le final le contraste
formé par ces différents thèmes dont on entend quelques
mesures et qui, enchâssés comme dans une fugue, finis-
sent par se fondre dans une synthèse de la forme sonate
et d'un art très rigoureux du contrepoint telle qu'on n'en
avait jamais connue, synthèse qui a profondément in-
fluencé Haydn lui-même et des générations entières de
compositeurs. Le fait que Mozart – il a déménagé six fois
depuis 1782 – change trois fois de domicile entre décembre 1787 et le début 1789, donne à penser qu'il connais-
sait une situation financière difficile. En juin 1788, soit
quelques mois après la naissance de son quatrième
enfant (qui, comme le premier et le troisième, meurt
dans sa première année), Mozart, qui travaille aux trois
dernières symphonies, demande à son ami et frère de
loge Michael Puchberg de lui consentir un prêt sur une
durée assez longue, démarche qui sera suivie d'autres
lettres de sollicitation. Le montant des sommes plus ou
moins substantielles avec lesquelles Puchberg lui vient
en aide au cours des années suivantes, s'élève à plus de
1400 florins. Ses revenus annuels fixes plafonnent en revanche aux seuls 800 florins qu'il perçoit depuis 1787 en
qualité de «compositeur de la cour royale et impériale»,
salaire auquel est uniquement liée l'obligation de fournir
des danses pour les bals masqués de la cour de Vienne.

Après la mort de l'empereur et la nomination de son
successeur Léopold II, la spirale de dettes s'emballe. Si
Mozart reste compositeur de la cour, il ne reçoit plus de
commandes. Tandis que sa femme tente de reprendre le
contrôle de la situation financière par un rééchelonnement,
il se rend à Francfort pour le couronnement de l'empereur. Mais comme il ne fait pas partie du train des 15 musiciens de la chambre impériale qui accompagnent Léopold II, il doit mettre en gage sa vaisselle en argent pour
financer le voyage. Ce qui fut un mauvais calcul. Le seul
concert qui a lieu à Francfort est «formidable du point de
vue de l'honneur, mais maigre en ce qui concerne l'argent».

Emanuel Schikaneder (1751–1812), Textdichter von „Die Zauberflöte" und „Eine
kleine Freimaurerkantate". Nach Jahren
glänzender Theatererfolge verliert er die
Gunst des Publikums und stirbt als
armer Mann. Punktierstich von Philipp
Richter, um 1810

Emanuel Schikaneder (1751–1812). Lib-
rettist of "Die Zauberflöte" and "Eine
kleine Freimaurerkantate." After years of
brilliant theatrical successes, he lost fav-
or with the public and died a poor man.
Stippled etching by Philipp Richter,
c. 1810

Emanuel Schikaneder (1751–1812),
auteur du livret de «La Flûte enchantée»
et d'«Une petite cantate franc-maçon-
nique». Après des années de brillants
succès au théâtre, le public se désintéres-
sera de lui. Il mourra dans la pauvreté.
Gravure pointillée de Philipp Richter,
vers 1810

Die Königin der Nacht in der
„Zauberflöte". Bühnenbildentwurf
von Simon Quaglio, München, 1818

The Queen of the Night, from "Die
Zauberflöte." Proposal for stage
setting by Simon Quaglio, Munich,
1818

La Reine de la Nuit dans « La Flûte
enchantée ». Décor de théâtre conçu
par Simon Quaglio, Munich, 1818

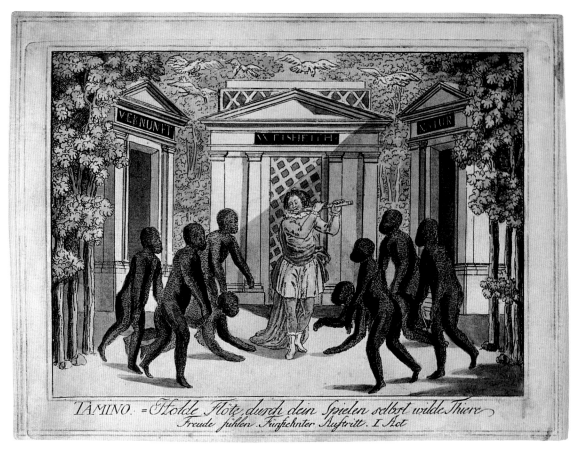

TAMINO. = *Holde Flöte, durch dein Spielen selbst wilde Thiere Freude fühlen. Fünfzehnter Auftritt. I Act*

Szenenbild der Uraufführung von „Die Zauberflöte" in Wien am 30. September 1791: „Holde Flöte, durch dein Spielen selbst wilde Thiere Freude fühlen" (1. Akt, 15. Szene). Die Tempelarchitektur und die Losung „Vernunft, Weisheit, Natur" verweisen auf den freimaurerischen Hintergrund der Zauberflöte. Mozarts letzte Oper ist das auf Anhieb erfolgreichste und im deutschsprachigen Raum bis heute meistgespielte seiner Bühnenwerke.

Stage setting for the premier of "Die Zauberflöte" in Vienna, September 30, 1791: "Noble Flute, through your music even wild animals feel joy" (Act I, scene 15). The temple architecture and the motto "Reason, Wisdom, Nature" are references to the "Zauberflöte's" Masonic background. Mozart's last opera was from the start his most successful, and is still today the most-often performed of his works in German-speaking countries.

Illustration d'une scène de la première de «La Flûte enchantée» à Vienne le 30 septembre 1791: «Noble flûte, grâce à ta musique, même les animaux sauvages éprouvent de la joie» (Acte I, scène 15). Le temple et la maxime «Raison, Sagesse, Nature» indiquent le fond maçonnique de «La Flûte enchantée». Le dernier opéra de Mozart connaîtra un succès immédiat, le plus grand jusqu'ici, et c'est lui qui sera le plus souvent joué dans les pays de langue allemande.

Eigenhändige Skizze von Johann Wolfgang von Goethe, der „Die Zauberflöte" am 16. Januar 1794 in Weimar herausbringt und sich ernsthaft mit einer Fortdichtung des Librettos befaßt („Der Zauberflöte zweiter Teil", Fragment). Zu den Bewunderern der „Zauberflöte" gehört auch Antonio Salieri. Mozart steht mit ihm in einen Konkurrenzverhältnis, das jedoch von gegenseitigem Respekt getragen ist. Gegen Ende seines Lebens wird Salieris Name in die Giftmord-Legende um Mozarts Tod verwoben und geht als der eines Mörders in die Theatergeschichte ein. Der Rufmord an Salieri in Alexander Puschkins Drama „Mozart und Salieri" (1832) findet Nachahmer, zuletzt 1984 in Milos Formans „Amadeus"-Film.

Sketches drawn by Johann Wolfgang von Goethe, who produced "Die Zauberflöte" in Weimar in 1794, and earnestly took up the continuation of the libretto ("The Magic Flute, second part"; fragment). The admirers of the "Zauberflöte" also included Antonio Salieri. The relationship between Mozart and Salieri was competitive, but characterized by mutual respect. Toward the end of his life, Salieri's name was woven into the legend of Mozart's supposed death by poisoning, and has come down in theater history as that of a murderer. The character assassination of Salieri carried out by Alexander Pushkin's in his drama "Mozart and Salieri" (1832) has found imitators, most recently Milos Forman's film "Amadeus" from 1984.

Croquis de la main de Johann Wolfgang von Goethe, qui fait paraître « La Flûte enchantée » à Weimar le 16 janvier 1794 et travaille sérieusement à une suite du livret (« La Flûte enchantée », seconde partie, fragment). Antonio Salieri compte lui aussi parmi les admirateurs de « La Flûte enchantée ». Mozart et lui sont concurrents mais éprouvent du respect l'un pour l'autre. A la fin de sa vie, la rumeur prétendra que Salieri a empoisonné Mozart et c'est sous les traits d'un meurtrier qu'il entrera dans l'histoire. La nouvelle d'Alexandre Pouchkine « Mozart et Salieri » (1832), dont Rimski-Korsakov tirera un opéra du même nom (1898), entretient cette réputation, reprise au cinéma par Milos Forman dans son film « Amadeus » en 1984.

Das Klavier als Lebenskunst

The Piano as the Art of Living

Das Klavier, auf dem er schon als Siebenjähriger alles „vom blat wek" spielt, ist Mozarts Erfolgsinstrument. Das Klavier ist Teil seiner Biographie und künstlerischen Identität, es ist seine Eintrittskarte in die Welt der Musik und für lange Zeit sein Lebensunterhalt. Die meisten der überlieferten Porträts zeigen Mozart an oder mit einem ‚Clavier' (in der Regel handelt es sich um ein Cembalo, das erst allmählich durch das Hammerklavier, den Vorläufer des modernen Flügels, verdrängt wird). Auch in den Jahren seiner großen Opernerfolge tritt es nicht völlig in den Hintergrund.

Noch 1788, vor Anbruch der letzten Lebensphase, versucht Mozart, sich von drückenden Existenzsorgen zu befreien und als Klaviervirtuose an frühere Triumphe anzuknüpfen – vergeblich. Das Wunderkind, das er einmal war, ist in Vergessenheit geraten, verblaßt ist auch der Glanz der ersten Wiener Jahre, in denen er als Hauptattraktion und Veranstalter eigener Konzerte aufgetreten war. Es sind diese ‚Akademien', für die Mozart zwischen 1784 und 1786 den bedeutendsten Teil seiner insgesamt etwa zwei Dutzend Klavierkonzerte komponierte. Nicht alle sind Meilensteine der Klavierkunst, zumal die frühen Werke nicht, die er als Elf- bzw. Sechzehnjähriger nach dem Vorbild von Komponisten wie Johann Christian Bach oder Johann Schobert schrieb. Aber schon die Salzburger Werke der siebziger Jahre zeigen, daß Mozart die Gattung des Klavierkonzerts nicht mehr als reine Gesellschaftskunst oder gefällige Konversation am Klavier versteht, sondern als Experimentierfeld seiner künstlerischen Ideen. Daß er im Es-Dur-Konzert (1777, KV 271, „Jeunehomme") das Soloinstrument bereits in die klassische Orchesterexposition eingreifen läßt und im zweiten Satz einen tiefernsten, nachgerade trauerumflorten Ton anschlägt, bedeutet einen Bruch mit konventioneller Glätte, auch wenn er sich vom Grundgestus der Eleganz und perlenden Geläufigkeit niemals weit entfernt.

Charakteristisch und für die Wiedergabe seiner Werke unabdingbar sind die improvisatorischen Elemente in den Klavierkonzerten. Sie beschränken sich nicht auf die Einfügung von frei auszugestaltenden Kadenzen am Satzende, zu ergänzen sind auch eine

The piano, the instrument on which Mozart even as a seven-year-old child already played everything directly at sight, remained the instrument of his success. The piano is a part of Mozart's biography and his artistic identity; it acted as his admission ticket into the world of music, and remained the basis of his livelihood through the years. Most surviving portraits depict Mozart either at or with a "clavier" (as a rule, the instrument is a cembalo, which was only gradually being replaced by the hammerclavier). Even in the years of his great operatic successes, the piano never wholly receded into the background.

Three years before his death, in 1788, Mozart attempted to free himself from the oppressive worries of earning a living by returning to his earlier triumphs as a piano virtuoso—but in vain. The erstwhile child prodigy had fallen into oblivion, just as the glory of the early years in Vienna, when Mozart had stepped onto the stage as the organizer and chief attraction of his own concerts, also paled. For these self-organized subscription concerts Mozart had composed the most significant portion of his approximately two dozen piano concertos between 1784 and 1786. Not all of them are milestones of the art of the piano, particularly not the early works that he had written as a boy following the model of composers like Johann Christian Bach or Johann Schobert. But Mozart's Salzburg compositions of the 1770s indicate that he no longer understood the genre of piano concerto as a merely social art, but as an experimental field for his artistic ideas. The Concerto in E-flat Major (K 271, 1777) already allowed the solo instrument to intrude into the classical orchestral exposition and, in the second movement, to strike a deep, truly sorrow-dimmed tone. These developments constituted a break with conventional balance and smoothness, although Mozart in fact never really wandered very far from a basic elegance of gesture and pearl-like fluency.

Characteristic of Mozart's works, and essential for performance, are the improvisational elements in the piano concertos, which are not limited to the insertion of cadences to be freely played by the pianist at the end of a movement. Also required are the expansion of a

Le piano, un art de vivre

Le piano, dont il joue dès l'âge de sept ans, est l'instrument du succès de Mozart. Il est partie intégrante de sa biographie et de son identité artistique, c'est son passeport pour l'univers musical et pendant longtemps, le moyen de gagner sa vie. La plupart des portraits qui nous sont parvenus de Mozart le montrent devant ou à côté d'un « clavier » (il s'agit en principe d'un clavecin, qui n'est que progressivement remplacé par le « Hammerklavier », l'ancêtre du piano à queue moderne). Même quand ses opéras lui vaudront de brillants succès, le piano ne disparaîtra jamais totalement.

En 1788, c'est-à-dire avant qu'il entame la dernière période de sa vie, Mozart essaie encore de se libérer de l'oppression des soucis matériels et, en sa qualité de virtuose du piano, de renouer avec ses succès d'antan. Mais en vain. L'enfant prodige qu'il a été est tombé dans l'oubli et l'éclat des premières années viennoises, où il faisait figure de principale attraction en organisant ses propres concerts, s'est lui aussi terni. C'est pour ces « académies » que Mozart a composé, entre 1784 et 1786, la majeure partie de ses concertos pour piano, qui sont au nombre d'une bonne vingtaine. Tous ne sont pas des chefs-d'œuvre d'un point de vue pianistique, et sûrement pas les premiers, écrits entre onze et seize ans d'après le modèle de compositeurs comme Jean Christian Bach ou Johann Schobert. Mais les œuvres salzbourgeoises des années soixante-dix montrent que Mozart ne conçoit déjà plus le genre du concerto pour piano comme un art de société ou une agréable causerie au clavier, mais comme un champ d'expérimentation de ses idées artistiques. Le fait que, dans le concerto de 1777 en mi bémol majeur, dit « Jeunehomme » (K. 271), il fasse intervenir l'instrument concertant dès la classique exposition de l'orchestre et que le second mouvement se concentre sur une sonorité grave d'où émane une profonde affliction, représente une rupture avec le côté lisse traditionnellement attaché au genre, même si le fond d'élégance et le pétillement d'usage ne sont jamais très loin.

Une des caractéristiques des concertos pour piano, et dont l'interprétation ne saurait faire l'économie, réside dans les éléments d'improvisation. Ceux-ci ne se limitent pas à l'insertion en fin de phrases de cadences

Einlaßkarte zu einer Mozart-Akademie in Wien, um 1785. Ursprünglich eine antike Philosophenschule, steht der Begriff ‚Akademie' bald allgemein für eine Vereinigung von Kunstliebhabern. Zur Zeit der Wiener Klassik werden auch Subskriptionskonzerte als Akademien bezeichnet.

Admission ticket to a subscription concert (called an "Academy") by Mozart in Vienna, c. 1785. Originally an ancient school of philosophers, the term "academy" came to stand in general for an association of art lovers. At the time of the Classical period in Vienna, the term also designated private concerts paid for by admission fees, i. e., by "subscription."

Billet d'entrée à une académie Mozart à Vienne, vers 1785. Si l'académie était dans l'Antiquité une école de philosophie, elle sera bientôt perçue en général comme une association d'amateurs d'art. A l'époque classique, les Viennois désignent aussi sous le nom d'« académies » les concerts à souscription.

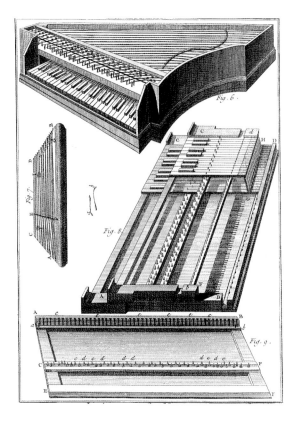

Abbildungen zum Bau von Saiteninstrumenten. Kupferstich aus der „Encyclopédie" oder „Dictionnaire raisonné des Sciences, des Arts et des Métiers", von Diderot/d'Alembert (1751–1772)
Seite 69: Mozart am Klavier. Unvollendetes Gemälde von Mozarts Schwager, dem Hofschauspieler Joseph Lange, 1789

Illustration of the construction of a plucked or struck stringed instrument. Copperplate engraving from Diderot and d'Alembert's Encyclopédie or *Dictionnaire raisonné des Sciences, des Arts et des Métiers,* (1751–1772).
Page 69: Mozart at the piano. Unfinished painting by Mozart's brother-in-law, the court actor, Joseph Lange, 1789

Illustrations décrivant la construction d'instruments à cordes. Eau-forte de l'« Encyclopédie », ou « Dictionnaire raisonné des Sciences, des Arts et des Métiers », publication (1751–1772) dirigée par Diderot et d'Alembert.
Page 69 : Mozart au piano. Tableau non achevé du beau-frère de Mozart, Joseph Lange, comédien au théâtre de la cour, 1789

Vielzahl von Verzierungen und sogenannte Eingänge, die zum eigentlichen Klaviereinsatz hinleiten, in der Partitur aber nicht fixiert sind. Wissen muß man auch, daß Mozart als Solist vom Klavier aus dirigierte und in traditioneller, noch aus der Barockzeit herrührender Praxis das Orchester mit Stützakkorden begleitete; auch dieser ‚Generalbaß' ist in der Partitur nicht ausnotiert.

Zu den faszinierendsten Aspekten seiner Arbeit gehören die Wechselwirkungen zwischen Instrumental- und Opernschaffen. In den Klavierkonzerten der Wiener Jahre korrespondieren beide Sphären so lebhaft miteinander, daß man im D-Moll-Konzert (1785, KV 466) eine nicht nur in der Grundtonart greifbare Verwandtschaft mit „Don Giovanni" und im A-Dur-Konzert (1786, KV 488) einen Widerschein des „Figaro" verspürt. Ein düsteres Gegenbild dazu ist das von Resignation umwitterte C-Moll-Konzert (KV 491), dessen sinfonische Gestaltung und opulente Orchesterbesetzung das herkömmliche Konzertschema in Frage stellt.

variety of ornaments and so-called introductions which lead to the actual entry of the piano, but which are not prescribed by the score. Mozart as soloist also directed the orchestra from the piano and, according to traditional practice stemming from the baroque, accompanied the orchestra with supporting chords; this basso continuo is also not written into the score.

Among the fascinating aspects of Mozart's work is the reciprocity between his instrumental and operatic composition process. In the piano concertos of the Viennese years, the two musical spheres correspond with each other in such a lively fashion that one discerns the palpable relation between the Concerto in D Minor (1785, K 466) and "Don Giovanni"—and not only in their sharing of a basic key. Similarly, one detects a reflection of "Figaro" in the Concert in A Major (1786, K 488). A dark reverse image of this correspondence is found in the C Minor Concerto (K 491), shrouded as it is with resignation, whose symphonic organization together with the

„Amadeus" am Klavier. Szenenfoto aus dem gleichnamigen Film von Milos Forman mit Tom Hulce in der Titelrolle (1984). Die Außenaufnahmen für den Film entstanden in der Altstadt-Kulisse von Prag. Die Vorlage für das Drehbuch lieferte ein Theaterstück von Peter Shaffer, dessen ‚Clou' die unsterbliche Giftmord-Hypothese ist.

"Amadeus" at the piano. Photograph of a scene from the film of the same name by Milos Forman, with Tom Hulce in the title role (1984). The old city center of Prague was the stage setting for the exterior scenes of the film. The basis of the script was a stage work by Peter Shaffer, whose theme is the eternal theory of death by poison.

« Amadeus » au piano. Photo d'une scène du film du même nom de Milos Forman avec Tom Hulce dans le rôle principal (1984). Les scènes d'extérieur ont été tournées dans la vieille ville de Prague. Le scénario est tiré d'une pièce de Peter Shaffer, centrée sur la théorie de l'empoisonnement, une hypothèse qui, apparemment, a la vie dure.

Glenn Gould (1932–1982) am Klavier. Der kanadische Pianist gilt als einer der bedeutendsten Interpreten der Klaviersonaten Mozarts, obwohl er von dessen Kompositionen im allgemeinen – und im besonderen von den Klavierkonzerten – nicht viel hielt: „Für mich besteht die G-Moll-Sinfonie aus acht bemerkenswerten Takten ... von einer halben Stunde Banalität umgeben."

Glenn Gould (1932–1982) at the piano. The Canadian pianist stands as one of the most important interpreters of Mozart's piano sonatas – although he did not think highly of Mozart's compositions in general, and in particular not the piano sonatas. "For me, the G-Minor Symphony consists of eight odd measures ... surrounded by a half an hour of banality."

Glenn Gould (1932–1982) au piano. Le pianiste canadien est considéré comme l'un des interprètes majeurs des sonates au piano de Mozart, bien qu'il n'ait pas fait grand cas de ses compositions en général, et des concerts au piano en particulier: «Pour moi la Symphonie en sol mineur, ce sont huit mesures remarquables... entourées d'une demi-heure de banalités. »

Mozarts Schwester Maria Anna ist eine hochbegabte Pianistin, doch durch ihre Heirat mit einem älteren Witwer übernimmt sie Erziehungspflichten für fünf Stiefkinder und tritt als Künstlerin nicht mehr öffentlich in Erscheinung. Gemälde von unbekannter Hand (Kopie), um 1785

Mozart's sister Maria Anna was a highly talented pianist, but with her marriage to an older widower, she took on the duties of raising five step-children, and no longer appeared publicly. Painting by unknown artist (copy), c. 1785

Maria Anna, la sœur de Mozart, est une pianiste de grand talent, mais elle épousera un veuf âgé, père de cinq enfants, dont elle devra assumer l'éducation, ce qui ne lui donnera plus guère le temps de se produire en public. Tableau peint par un artiste anonyme (copie), vers 1785

Als sich sein Ruhm als Opernkomponist in Wien und Prag gefestigt hat, beginnt Mozarts Stern als Pianist zu sinken. Das mag ihn bestimmt haben, mit dem auf älteren Skizzen beruhenden C-Dur-Konzert (1786, KV 503) wieder in geregeltere Bahnen einzuschwenken, aber gerade dieses Werk ist wohl weniger ein Beweis mangelnder Experimentierfreude als vielmehr Ausdruck eines abgeklärten Spätstils, der die stolze Reihe der Klavierkonzerte zu einem vorläufigen Abschluß bringt. Erst zwei Jahre später folgt das für eine nicht mehr zustandegekommene Wiener Akademie geplante D-Dur-Konzert (KV 537), ein seltsam uninspiriertes Werk, das Mozart anläßlich einer Deutschlandreise am Dresdner Hof und nochmals 1790 bei den Feiern zur Kaiserkrönung in Frankfurt präsentierte. Als letztes entsteht das B-Dur-Konzert (KV 595), das in der Beschränkung auf ein Orchester ohne Klarinetten, Pauken und Trompeten Empfindungen an der Grenze zur Entrückung auslotet; gebrochen wirkt auch die Heiterkeit des Schlußsatzes – eigentlich eine muntere ‚Chasse' (Jagdmusik) – mit dem Zitat des Liedes „Sehnsucht nach dem Frühling" (KV 596).

rich configuration of the orchestra throw the traditional concerto scheme into question.

As Mozart's star as an opera composer was rising in Vienna and Prague, his career as a pianist had passed its zenith. This may have determined him to swing again into more conventional tracks with the C-Major Concerto (1786, K 503), which was based on older sketches. But precisely this work is probably less an indication of dwindling joy in experimentation than an expression of a serene late style, which marked a temporary end to the splendid series of piano concerts. Not until two years later did Mozart compose the Concerto in D Major (K 537), a singularly uninspired work, originally conceived for a Viennese subscription concert that never took place. The last to be composed was the B Major Concerto (K 595), whose limitation of the orchestra (it lacks clarinets, drums and trumpets) plumbs sensations bordering literally on ex-stase, a state of being outside itself, outside the concerto tradition. The ostensible brightness of the final movement seems also to dissolve with the citation of the song, "Longing for Spring" (K 596).

confiées à la libre inspiration de l'exécutant ; il faut en effet y ajouter une multiplicité d'ornements et ce qu'on appelle les entrées, qui amènent l'attaque du piano proprement dite mais ne sont pas fixées dans la partition. Il faut savoir également que Mozart, en tant que soliste, dirigeait depuis le piano et, suivant une pratique traditionnelle, accompagnait encore l'orchestre par des accords qui lui servaient d'appuis ; cette « basse générale » n'est pas non plus notée dans la partition.

Les interactions entre la création instrumentale et la création lyrique comptent parmi les aspects les plus fascinants de son travail. Dans les concertos pour piano de la période viennoise, les deux sphères communiquent avec une telle vivacité qu'on a l'impression, dans le concerto en ré mineur (1785, K. 466), de trouver une parenté avec « Don Giovanni », parenté qui du reste ne se limite pas à la seule tonalité de base, et d'entendre dans le concerto en la majeur (1786, K. 488) un écho de « Figaro ». On se trouve en présence d'un sombre contre-exemple avec la résignation dans laquelle baigne le concerto en ut mineur (K. 491), dont l'organisation symphonique et la richesse de l'orchestre remettent en question le schéma traditionnel du concerto.

La consécration de Mozart à Vienne et à Prague en tant que compositeur d'opéras va de pair avec le déclin de son étoile de pianiste. C'est peut-être ce qui l'a déterminé à emprunter des voies plus balisées avec le concerto en ut majeur (1786, K. 503). Bien que reposant sur des ébauches assez anciennes, cette œuvre est pourtant bien moins la preuve d'un manque de plaisir à expérimenter que l'expression d'une maturité stylistique qui met un terme provisoire à la fière série des concertos pour piano. Mais deux ans plus tard, Mozart compose déjà le concerto en ré majeur (K. 537), une œuvre curieusement peu inspirée qu'il présente à l'occasion d'un voyage en Allemagne à la cour de Dresde, et, en 1790 à Francfort, le concerto en si bémol majeur (K. 595), pour les festivités du couronnement de l'empereur – d'où le nom de « concerto du couronnement ». Dans le dernier, le dépouillement de l'orchestre qu'ont déserté clarinettes, timbales et trompettes fait sourdre des sensations qui confinent au ravissement ; la citation du lied « Nostalgie du printemps » (K. 596) dans le mouvement final, qui est par ailleurs une joyeuse musique de chasse, concourt également à en briser la sérénité.

Die Mozart-Söhne Franz Xaver und Carl Thomas. Gemälde von Hans Hansen, um 1798

The Mozarts' sons, Franz Xaver and Carl Thomas. Painting by Hans Hansen, c. 1798

Les fils de Mozart, Franz Xaver et Carl Thomas. Tableau de Hans Hansen, vers 1798

Tod und Verklärung

Aus Frankfurt zurückgekehrt, findet Mozart die Einladung eines englischen Konzertagenten vor, der ihm für die Komposition zweier Opern und Auftritte in London annähernd 2500 Gulden in Aussicht stellt. Anders als der schon fast sechzigjährige Joseph Haydn, dem ebenfalls eine Einladung aus London vorliegt, schlägt Mozart das glänzende Angebot aus, vielleicht mit Rücksicht auf den Gesundheitszustand seiner Frau. Ende 1789 hat sie ihr fünftes Kind zur Welt gebracht, ein Mädchen, das schon eine Stunde nach der Geburt stirbt; 1791 ist sie schwanger mit dem sechsten und muß sich wegen eines langwierigen Fußleidens zum wiederholten Mal einer Kur in Baden bei Wien unterziehen. Von Anfang Juni bis Mitte Juli ist sie dort, begleitet von ihrem inzwischen sechsjährigen Sohn Carl Thomas. Mozart bleibt in Wien, doch besucht er seine Frau gelegentlich; das Geld für ihren Baden-Aufenthalt muß er sich bei Freunden borgen. Am 11. Juni schreibt er ihr: „Aus lauter langer Weile habe ich heute von der Oper eine Arie componirt", gemeint ist „Die Zauberflöte", die ihn seit dem Frühjahr beschäftigt. Urheber der Idee und Hauptlieferant des Textes ist Emanuel Schikaneder, Pächter des Freihaustheaters auf der Wieden in der Wiener Vorstadt. Mozart steht mit ihm noch aus Salzburger Tagen auf freundschaftlichem Fuß. Schikaneder, als Schauspieler und Stückeschreiber ein Liebling des Wiener Publikums, ist ein Theatermann mit Leib und Seele und untrüglichem Gespür für spektakuläre Effekte. Als der berühmte Ballonfahrer François Blanchard im Juli 1791 erstmals im Prater aufsteigt, baut Schikaneder sogleich eine Ballonfahrt in die Bühnenhandlung der „Zauberflöte" ein.

Platteste Publikumsbelustigung oder freimaurerisch inspiriertes Ideendrama? – „Die Zauberflöte" läßt beide Deutungen zu. Die krassen dramaturgischen Brüche und Merkwürdigkeiten des Textbuchs haben den auf Anhieb überragenden Erfolg der Oper jedenfalls nicht behindert. Daß sich dieser Erfolg im wesentlichen der Musik verdankt, beweist nur, wie unbefangen Mozart sich dem Schikanederschen Bühnenspektakel genähert und welch ungeheure Inspiration er daraus gezogen hat.

Death and Transfiguration

Upon his return from Frankfurt, Mozart was greeted by the invitation of an English concert agent awaiting him, who held out the prospect of nearly 2,500 gulden for the composition of two operas and appearances in London. Unlike the almost sixty-year-old Joseph Haydn, who had also received an invitation from London, Mozart rejected the brilliant offer out of hand, perhaps because of his wife's health. Constanze had given birth to their fifth child at the end of 1789, a girl, who lived only an hour; now, in 1791, Constanze was pregnant again, and needed another cure for a protracted foot problem. The weeks from early June until mid-August she spent at the health spa of Baden near Vienna, accompanied by their six-year-old son Carl Thomas. Mozart remained in the city, paying occasional visits to his wife. The money for the cure had to be borrowed from friends. On June 11 he wrote to her that, "Out of pure excess of leisure, today I composed an aria from the opera." He was referring to "Die Zauberflöte" ("The Magic Flute") on which he had been working since the spring. Mastermind of the idea and chief author of the text was Emanuel Schikaneder, who held the lease for the Freihaustheater auf der Wieden outside the city limits of Vienna. Mozart had been on friendly terms with him since his Salzburg days. Schikaneder, a favorite actor and playwright of the Viennese public, was body and soul a man of the theater, and possessed an unerring sense for spectacular effects. In July 1791, when the famed balloonist François Blanchard took off for the first time from the Prater, Schikaneder immediately incorporated a balloon trip into the stage action of the "Zauberflöte".

The most trivial popular entertainment or a Masonic-inspired drama of ideas? "Die Zauberflöte" admits of both interpretations. In any case, right from the start, the blatant dramaturgic interruptions and oddities of the libretto never interfered with the opera's overwhelming success. That this success is primarily due to the music only proves how unreservedly Mozart accepted Schikaneder's stage spectacle and what immense inspiration he drew from it.

The summer of 1791 brought an improvement in the Mozarts' financial situation, for even as the compo-

Mort et transfiguration

De retour de Francfort, Mozart trouve l'invitation d'un organisateur de concerts anglais qui lui fait entrevoir une somme d'environ 2500 florins pour qu'il compose deux opéras et donne quelques concerts à Londres. A la différence de Haydn qui, tandis qu'il a déjà presque soixante ans, est lui aussi invité à Londres, Mozart décline cette offre miroitante, peut-être par égard pour l'état de santé de sa femme. Fin 1789, celle-ci a mis au monde son cinquième enfant, une fille qui meurt une heure seulement après sa naissance; en 1791, elle se trouve de nouveau enceinte du sixième et doit se résigner à partir en cure à Baden, près de Vienne, pour une affection du pied dont elle souffre depuis longtemps. Elle s'y trouve de début juin à la mi-juillet, en compagnie de son fils Carl Thomas alors âgé de seize ans. Mozart reste à Vienne mais rend de temps en temps visite à sa femme. Quant à l'argent nécessaire à son séjour à Baden, il lui faut l'emprunter à des amis. Il écrit le 11 juin à Constance : « Aujourd'hui je m'ennuyais, alors j'ai composé un air de l'opéra », sous-entendu « La Flûte enchantée », qui l'occupe depuis le printemps. L'idée et la majeure partie du texte sont dues à Emanuel Schikaneder, directeur du « Freihaustheater auf der Wieden », théâtre d'un faubourg de Vienne, avec lequel Mozart était déjà en bons termes à Salzbourg. Schikaneder, qui en tant qu'acteur et auteur dramatique est la coqueluche du public viennois, est un homme que le théâtre habite corps et âme et qui de plus, a un sens infaillible des effets spectaculaires. Lorsque le ballon du célèbre aéronaute François Blanchard s'élève pour la première fois au-dessus du Prater en juillet 1791, Schikaneder insère aussitôt un voyage en ballon dans l'action de la « Flûte enchantée ».

Banal divertissement populaire ou théâtre d'idées d'inspiration maçonnique ? « La Flûte enchantée » se prête aux deux interprétations. Les ruptures prononcées de la dramaturgie et les singularités du livret n'ont en tout cas pas empêché que, contre toute attente, le succès se fasse immédiatement sentir. Le fait que ce succès soit essentiellement dû à la musique prouve simplement l'absence de préjugés avec laquelle Mozart a abordé le spectacle scénique de Schikaneder et la formidable inspiration qu'il en a reçue.

Mozart-Kupferstich nach einer Silberstiftzeichnung von Dorothea Stock, Dresden, 1789

Copperplate engraving of Mozart, from a silver pencil drawing by Dorothea Stock, Dresden, 1789

Eau-forte représentant Mozart d'après un dessin à la mine d'argent de Dorothea Stock, Dresde, 1789

Mozart-Silhouette, gestochen von Hieronymus Löschenkohl, 1786
Seite 77: Ballonfahrt in Ingmar Bergmans Verfilmung der „Zauberflöte" (1975): „Drei Knäbchen, jung, schön, hold und weise, umschweben euch auf eurer Reise ..."

Silhouette of Mozart, engraved by Hieronymus Löschenkohl, 1786
Page 77: Balloon trip from Ingmar Bergman's filming of "Die Zauberflöte" (1975): "Three little boys, young, fair, sweet and wise, will hover above you on your journey ..."

Silhouette de Mozart gravée par Hieronymus Löschenkohl, 1786
Page 77 : Voyage en ballon dans l'adaptation cinématographique d'Ingmar Bergman de « La Flûte enchantée » (1975) : « Trois garçonnets, jeunes, beaux, doux et sages, volettent autour de vous durant votre voyage... »

Im Sommer 1791 zeichnet sich eine Besserung seiner finanziellen Lage ab, denn noch während der Arbeit an der „Zauberflöte" erhält Mozart zwei lukrative Kompositionsaufträge. Der erste kommt aus Prag, wo man sich eine Festoper von ihm wünscht, geschrieben auf ein klassisches, bereits etliche Male vertontes Libretto von Pietro Metastasio („La clemenza di Tito"). Aufgeführt werden soll sie am 6. September im Nationaltheater zu Ehren Leopolds II., der an diesem Tag die böhmische Königskrone empfängt. Mozart braucht weniger als drei Wochen für die Komposition, allerdings überläßt er das Ausschreiben der Rezitative einem seiner Schüler, wahrscheinlich Franz Xaver Süßmayr, der ihn und seine Frau nach Prag begleitet. Der im Juli geborene Franz Xaver Wolfgang wird vorübergehend in Pflege gegeben, der ältere Sohn, Carl Thomas, in einem Internat untergebracht.

Auch wenn es Mozart zusammen mit dem sächsischen Hofdichter Caterino Mazzolà, der den Metastasio-Text bearbeitet, gelingt, das vorgegebene ‚seria'-Korsett mit seiner starren Abfolge von Rezitativen und Arien durch Ensembleszenen zu lockern und den papierenen Gestalten dieser Huldigungsoper so etwas wie Leben einzuhauchen, wird „Titus" kein Erfolg. Das Herrscherpaar verspätet sich zur Aufführung und zeigt auch sonst alle Anzeichen von Mißvergnügen: „una porcheria tedesca" (eine deutsche Schweinerei) soll die aus Neapel stammende Kaiserin gerufen haben. Im Gegensatz zum Premierenpublikum honoriert Mozarts bürgerliche Anhängerschaft, die die folgenden Aufführungen besucht, das Werk „mit außerordentlichen beifall".

Der zweite große Auftrag des Sommers 1791, ein „Requiem" (KV 626), bleibt wegen der Arbeit an der Titus-Oper liegen. Um die Entstehung dieses Requiems rankt sich die Legende, daß ein geheimnisvoller ‚grauer Bote' den Auftrag überbrachte und Mozart in ihm den Verkünder seines nahen Todes sah. Tatsächlich hieß der Auftraggeber, auch wenn er selbst wohl nicht namentlich in Erscheinung trat, Franz Graf von Walsegg-Stuppach, ein musikbegeisterter Adliger, dem es offenbar gefiel, anonym, das heißt über Mittelsmänner, Kompositionen zu erwerben und sie aufzuführen, mit dem Anschein, er selbst sei der Schöpfer dieser Werke. Zum Gedächtnis an seine im Februar verstorbene Frau hatte er sich ausgedacht, bei Mozart eine Seelenmesse zu bestellen.

ser was still working on the "Zauberflöte," he received
two other lucrative commissions for compositions. The
first stemmed from Prague, where patrons wished a festival opera to be composed for a classical libretto by
Pietro Metastasio ("La clemenza di Tito"), which had
already been set to music several times. Mozart's version
would be presented on September 6 in the National Theater of Prague in honor of the coronation of Leopold II as
king of Bohemia. Mozart needed less than three weeks
for the composition, but admittedly left the writing of
the recitative to one of his students, probably Franz
Xaver Süssmayr, who accompanied Mozart and Constanze to Prague. The new baby, Franz Xaver Wolfgang,
born in July, was sent out to nurse, and the older son,
Carl Thomas, was placed in a boarding school.

Although Mozart—together with Caterino Mazzolà, the court poet of Saxony, who was working on the
Metastasio text—succeeded in loosening the prescribed
seria corset with its fixed order of recitative and arias by
means of ensemble scenes, thus breathing a little spirit
into the lifeless characters of this opera in honor of the
newly-crowned king, "La clemenza di Tito" was not a
success. The royal couple arrived late at the performance
and otherwise showed all signs of displeasure, the
Naples-born empress supposedly shouting out *una porcheria tedesca* ("a swinish German mess"). In contrast to
the elevated public at the premier, however, Mozart's
bourgeois fans who attended the subsequent performances honored the work "with extraordinary applause."

Because of his work on the "Titus" opera, the second great commission of the summer of 1791, a requiem,
lay untouched. Legends surround the creation of this
"Requiem," (K 626), whose commission was reputedly
conveyed by a mysterious "gray messenger" in whom

Une amélioration de sa situation financière se pro-
file durant l'été 1791 où, tandis qu'il travaille à la « Flûte
enchantée », Mozart reçoit deux commandes lucratives.
La première vient de Prague, où on lui demande d'écrire,
sur un livret classique de Pierre Métastase (« La Clémence
de Titus »), un opéra dont la création aura lieu le 6 septembre au théâtre national en l'honneur de Léopold II,
qui doit ce jour-là être sacré roi de Bohême. Moins de
trois semaines sont nécessaires à Mozart pour cette
composition, même s'il confie l'écriture des récitatifs à
un de ses élèves, probablement Franz Xaver Süßmayr,
qui accompagne le couple à Prague. Franz Xaver Wolfgang, qui est né en juillet, est mis momentanément en
nourrice et le fils aîné, Carl Thomas, en pension.

Même si Mozart parvient, avec l'aide du poète de la
cour de Saxe Caterino Mazzolà qui adapte le texte de Métastase, à assouplir le carcan imposé de l'« opera seria »
en introduisant des scènes d'ensemble dans sa succession rigide de récitatifs et d'arias et à insuffler un sem-
blant de vie aux personnages de papier de cet opéra de
prestige, « Titus » n'est pas un succès. Le couple royal non
seulement est en retard à la représentation, mais il manifeste des signes de mécontentement. « Una porcheria
tedesca » (une cochonnerie tudesque), se serait même
exclamée l'impératrice, originaire de Naples. Contrai-
rement au public de la première, les partisans bourgeois
de Mozart vont aux représentations suivantes et ovation-
nent l'œuvre « de tonnerres d'applaudissements ».

La seconde grande commande de l'été 1791, un « requiem »(K. 626), est mise de côté pour travailler à Titus.
La légende qui s'est tissée autour de ce requiem veut que
la commande en ait été remise à Mozart par un mysté-
rieux « messager gris » en qui il aurait vu l'annonciateur
de sa mort prochaine. Le commanditaire, même s'il ne

Tom Hulce als Mozart und F. Murray Abraham als Salieri in Milos Formans Kinofilm „Amadeus". Der erfolgreichste Film des Jahres 1984 wurde mit acht Oscars ausgezeichnet. Auch im deutschsprachigen Kino begegnet uns Mozart als Held zweier Spielfilme des Regisseurs Karl Hartl („Wen die Götter lieben", 1942, und „Reich mir die Hand, mein Leben", 1955). Zu den bemerkenswertesten Verfilmungen von Mozarts Opern gehört neben Ingmar Bergmans „Die Zauberflöte" der 1979 entstandene „Don Giovanni" von Joseph Losey.

Tom Hulce as Mozart and F. Murray Abraham as Salieri in Milos Forman's film "Amadeus." The most successful film of 1984, it was crowned with eight Oscars. In German film also, Mozart appeared as the hero of two films by the director Karl Hartl—"Wen die Götter lieben" (Whom the gods love) in 1942 and "Reich mir die Hand, mein Leben" (Give me your hand, my dear) in 1955. Among the most remarkable filmings of Mozart's operas, in addition to Ingmar Bergman's "Die Zauberflöte" is Joseph Losey's "Don Giovanni" from 1979.

Tom Hulce interprète Mozart et F. Murray Abraham Salieri dans le film de Milos Forman «Amadeus», sorti en salle en 1984, qui obtiendra huit Oscars et battra les records d'entrée. Dans le cinéma allemand, Mozart est aussi le héros de deux films du réalisateur Karl Hartl («Wen die Götter lieben», 1942, et «Reich mir die Hand, mein Leben», 1955). A côté de «La Flûte enchantée» d'Ingmar Bergmann, le «Don Giovanni» de Joseph Losey, réalisé en 1979 est l'une des adaptations cinématographiques les plus remarquables des opéras de Mozart.

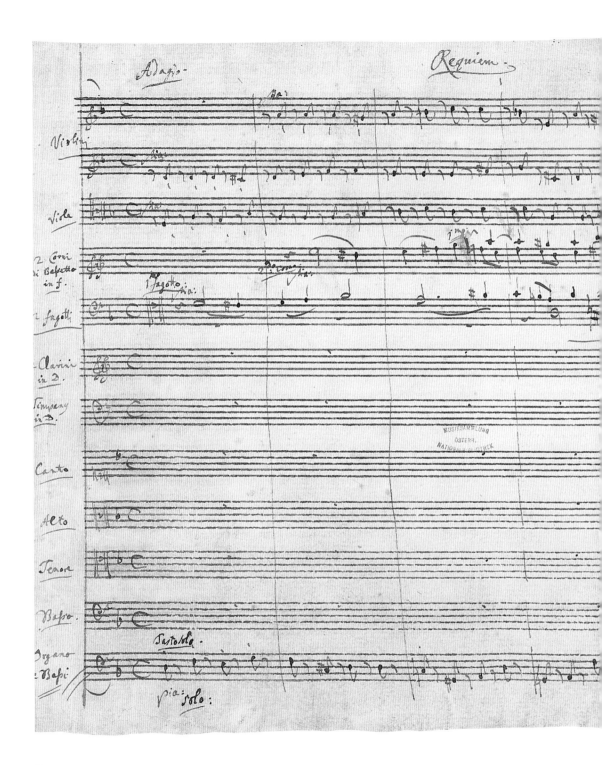

„Requiem", eigenhändige Notenhand-
schrift Mozarts, 1790

"Requiem," Mozart's score, 1790

«Requiem», partition de la main de
Mozart, 1790

81

Nikolaus Harnoncourt, einer der profi-
liertesten Mozart-Dirigenten unserer
Zeit, setzt der in modernen Orchestern
vorherrschenden Ästhetik des glatten
Schönklangs ein aus der Rückbesinnung
auf die originalen Instrumente und Be-
setzungen gewonnenes Klangideal der
extremen Ausdruckswerte entgegen.

Nikolaus Harnoncourt, one of the most
distinguished Mozart directors of our
times, counters the modern aesthetic of
the smooth and beautiful tone that pre-
dominates in today's symphonic orchestra with the historic sound ideal deriving
from a return to the original instrumentation and extreme expressive values.

Nikolaus Harnoncourt, un des chefs
d'orchestre les plus marquants de
l'œuvre mozartienne aujourd'hui, oppo-
se à l'esthétique du beau son lisse qui
domine dans les orchestres symphoni-
ques modernes un idéal sonore des va-
leurs expressives extrêmes qu'il obtient
en revenant aux instruments d'origine et
aux relations dans la distribution à
l'époque de Mozart.

Mozart ist 35 Jahre alt und hat eine Familie zu
versorgen. Nach einem Jahrzehnt als freischaffender
Künstler strebt er nun ein festes Amt an. Vom Magistrat
der Stadt hat er die Zusicherung erhalten, Nachfolger
des kränkelnden Domkapellmeisters an St. Stephan zu
werden, dem er bereits seit dem Frühjahr „unentgeltlich
adjungiret" ist. Es ist mit 2000 Gulden jährlich eine der
höchstbezahlten Positionen für einen Musiker in Wien.
In der Absicht, seine Einkommensverhältnisse ins Lot
zu bringen, scheint Mozart in bürgerliche Bahnen einzuschwenken, ohne seinem großzügigen, durchaus
bohèmehaften Lebensstil gänzlich abzuschwören. Aus
einer Geldverlegenheit heraus trennt er sich allerdings
von seinem Reitpferd. Frohgemut berichtet er seiner
Frau, nach ihrer Abreise am 7. Oktober 1791 habe er
„um 14 duckaten" seinen „kleper" verkauft; vorher hat
er noch zwei Partien Billard gespielt, danach läßt er sich
Kaffee holen, schmaucht dazu „eine herrliche Pfeiffe
toback" und instrumentiert „fast das ganze Rondó vom
Stadtler", den Schlußsatz des Klarinettenkonzerts KV
622 – ein Tagesbericht, der nicht das geringste Anzei-

Mozart saw the harbinger of his own approaching death.
The patron who commissioned the work, even though
his name remained hidden, was in fact Franz Count von
Walsegg-Stuppach, a nobleman and music enthusiast,
whom it evidently pleased to purchase compositions
anonymously, that is, through a middleman, and then to
present the works under the guise of his own author-
ship. In memory of his wife who had died in February,
the count had devised the plan of commissioning Mozart
with a mass for the dead.

Mozart was now thirty-five years old with a family
to support. After a decade as a free-lance artist, he applied
for a permanent appointment. He had received assurance from the city magistrate that he would be named
successor to the ailing cathedral *Kapellmeister* at St. Stephan's, where Mozart had already been in a position of
"unpaid association" since the spring. At 2,000 gulden
per year, the promised appointment was one of the
highest paid musical positions in Vienna. Intending to
bring his financial situation in order, Mozart seems to
have steered toward a bourgeois line without entirely

Elisa Müller als Sextus in Mozarts „La clemenza di Tito" (Breslau, 1805). Die Rolle des Sextus, eigentlich eine klassische Kastratenpartie und bei der Uraufführung auch als solche besetzt, wird schon bald nach Mozarts Tod zur ‚Hosenrolle', weil Kastraten nicht mehr zur Verfügung stehen.

Elisa Müller as Sextus in Mozart's "La clemenza di Tito" (Breslau, 1805). The roll of Sextus, in fact a classical castrato role, and played as such in the premier, was soon after Mozart's death made into a "breeches part," because castrati were no longer available.

Elisa Müller incarnant Sextus dans « La Clémence de Titus » (Breslau, 1805). Le rôle de Sextus, une partition destinée à un castrat et qui sera chantée par un castrat lors de la première, devient un rôle de femme peu de temps après la mort de Mozart, les castrats n'étant plus disponibles.

s'est pas nommément manifesté, était en réalité un comte du nom de Franz von Walsegg-Stuppach. C'était un aristocrate mélomane à qui il plaisait manifestement d'acquérir des œuvres de façon anonyme, c'est-à-dire en passant par des intermédiaires, et de les exécuter en laissant croire que lui-même en était l'auteur. Il avait imagine de commander à Mozart une messe des morts en mémoire de sa femme disparue en février.

Mozart a maintenant 35 ans et une famille à entretenir. Après dix années d'une vie d'artiste indépendant, il aspire à présent à un poste fixe. Il a obtenu de la municipalité l'assurance de prendre la succession du maître de chapelle de la cathédrale Saint-Etienne, dont la santé laisse à désirer, et auquel on l'a « adjoint bénévolement » depuis le printemps. Avec 2000 florins par an, il s'agit pour un musicien viennois d'un des postes les mieux rétribués. Mozart semble s'engager alors, dans l'intention de mettre de l'ordre dans ses revenus, sur une pente bourgeoise sans toutefois renoncer complètement à la largeur d'esprit et au côté bohème de son style de vie. Une gêne financière l'oblige toutefois à se séparer de

Représentation Théâtrale de la   IVme Scène du 1.^r
peinte par Fuentes pour le   Théâtre de Innocenti

„Titus"-Bühnenbildentwurf von Giorgio
Fuentes, Frankfurt, 19. Jahrhundert

Stage design for "Titus" by Giorgio
Fuentes, Frankfurt, 19th century

« La Clémence de Titus » – décor de scène
conçu par Giorgio Fuentes, Francfort,
19ᵉ siècle

Mozart auf dem Sterbelager, sein Requiem komponierend – eine romantisch
verklärende Sicht der letzten Lebensphase Mozarts. Gemälde von William
James Grant, Mitte des 19. Jahrhunderts.
Verbürgt ist, daß Mozart sich tatsächlich
noch auf dem Totenbett mit dem Requiem beschäftigte.

Mozart, composing his "Requiem" on
his deathbed—a romantic transfigura-
tion of the last phase of Mozart's life.
Painting by William James Grant, mid-
19th century.
The fact is that Mozart was indeed still at
work on the "Requiem" on his deathbed.

Mozart composant son Requiem sur son
lit de mort – une vision teintée de roman-
tisme des derniers moments de Mozart.
Tableau de William James Grant, milieu
du 19ᵉ siècle.
Il est néanmoins établi que Mozart tra-
vailla à son Requiem jusqu'à son dernier
souffle.

Mozart-Memorabilien: Einladung Konstanze Mozarts zu einem Konzert ihres jüngsten Sohnes im Jahr 1805, Mozarts letzte Kantate, eine Haarlocke Leopold Mozarts und ein Empfehlungsbrief Antonio Salieris. Der nach Mozarts Tod geschätzte Wert des Hausrats, der Kleidung und der Bücher beläuft sich auf nur 500 Gulden, unschätzbar hingegen ist der musikalische Nachlaß, den seine Witwe gemeinsam mit Georg Nikolaus von Nissen verwaltet. Konstanze Mozart stirbt 1842 als vermögende Frau.

Mozart memorabilia: An invitation of Constanze Mozart's to a concert of her youngest son in 1805; Mozart's last cantata; a lock of hair belonging to Leopold Mozart; and a letter of recommendation by Antonio Salieri. The estimated value of the household goods after Mozart's death, together with the clothing and books, amounted to only 500 gulden; in contrast, the musical estate that his widow administered together with Georg Nikolaus von Nissen, is invaluable. Constanze Mozart died a wealthy woman in 1842.

Souvenirs de Mozart: une invitation de Constance Mozart au concert de son plus jeune fils en 1805 ; la dernière cantate de Mozart, une boucle de cheveux ayant appartenu à Léopold Mozart et une lettre de recommandation d'Antonio Salieri. La valeur du mobilier, des vêtements et des livres, estimée après la mort de Mozart, ne s'élève qu'à 500 florins. En revanche l'héritage musical que sa veuve administrera avec Georg Nikolaus von Nissen est d'une valeur inestimable. Constance Mozart, qui mourra en 1842, est une femme riche.

Georg Nikolaus von Nissen (1761–1826), dänischer Diplomat. Porträt von Ferdinand Jagemann, 1809
Nissen, während seiner Zeit als Legationssekretär in Wien Untermieter von Konstanze Mozart, wird 1809 ihr zweiter Ehemann. Von 1810 bis 1820 leben beide in Kopenhagen, danach lassen sie sich in Salzburg nieder.

Georg Nikolaus von Nissen (1761–1826), Danish diplomat. Portrait by Ferdinand Jagemann, 1809
During his time as secretary of the Danish legation in Vienna, Nissen sublet an apartment from Konstanze Mozart; in 1809 he became her second husband. From 1810 to 1820, they lived in Copenhagen, then settled in Salzburg.

Georg Nikolaus von Nissen (1761–1826), diplomate danois. Portrait de Ferdinand Jagemann, 1809
Nissen, sous-locataire de Constance Mozart alors qu'il était secrétaire de légation à Vienne, épousera la veuve du musicien en 1809. Ils vivront de 1810 à 1820 à Copenhague, et s'installeront ensuite à Salzbourg.

chen nachlassender Lebens- oder Schaffensenergie erkennen läßt.

Im November, mitten in der Arbeit am Requiem, wird Mozart krank. Seine letzte vollendete Komposition ist „Eine kleine freymaurer-kantate" (KV 623), die er am 18. November in der Loge „Zur neugekrönten Hoffnung" dirigiert. Zwei Tage später wird er bettlägerig, sein Zustand verschlechtert sich rapide. Am 5. Dezember, fünf Minuten vor ein Uhr nachts, stirbt er im Beisein seiner Frau, seiner Schwägerin Sophie und seines Arztes Dr. Closset.

Über die Todesursache („hitziges Frieselfieber") ist viel gerätselt worden. Wahrscheinlich kommen mehrere Ursachen zusammen: ein durch Überarbeitung geschwächter Allgemeinzustand, eine rheumatische Entzündung, ausgelöst vielleicht durch das nachweislich schlechte Wetter, nicht zuletzt auch die nach dem damaligen Stand ärztlicher Kunst verordneten Aderlässe. Für die weit verbreitete Mär von einem Giftmord – eine der unsterblichen Mozart-Legenden – bieten die wenigen gesicherten Nachrichten über seine Todeskrankheit keinen Anhaltspunkt.

Ebenso unhaltbar ist die Behauptung, Mozart sei in einem Armengrab verscharrt worden. Wahr ist, daß sein Leichnam nach den damals geltenden Begräbnisvorschriften, die keinen Pomp gestatten, auf dem St. Marxer Friedhof beigesetzt wird. Weil der Friedhof einige Kilometer vor der Stadt liegt, ist es nicht üblich, daß die Trauergemeinde dem Sarg dorthin folgt, zumal die Überführung des Sarges – auch das entspricht den Vorschriften – erst nach sechs Uhr abends, also nach Einbruch der Dunkelheit, stattfindet. Die Grabstelle selbst bleibt anonym. Grabkreuze anzubringen, erlaubt die Begräbnisordnung nicht. Vorausgegangen ist eine Trauerfeier im Stephansdom. In Prag hält man schon eine Woche später einen Gedenkgottesdienst ab, an dem 4000 Menschen teilnehmen.

Mozarts Witwe bittet Franz Xaver Süßmayr, das Requiem fertigzustellen, denn der Auftraggeber hat bereits eine Anzahlung geleistet. Süßmayr komponiert die fehlenden Teile nach (Sanctus, Benedictus, Agnus Dei), ergänzt und orchestriert das, was er an Skizzen vorfindet, und greift für die Communio („Lux aeterna") auf Material des noch von Mozart vollendeten Introitus und Kyrie zurück. Als Konstanze Mozart das Werk später in Druck geben will, kommt es zu einer Auseinander-

renouncing his open-handed, thoroughly bohemian lifestyle. Admittedly, in the face of a financial embarrassment he gave up his riding horse, reporting confidently to his wife that after her departure on October 7, 1791, he had sold his "nag" for "14 ducats." Beforehand, he continued, he had played two games of billiards, then sent for coffee, smoked "a glorious pipe of tobacco" while he was drinking, and arranged "almost the complete rondo of Stadtler," that is, the final movement of the Clarinet Concerto (K 622)—a report of the day's activities that does not betray the least hint of the ebbing of life or creative energy.

In November, in the midst of working on the "Requiem," Mozart fell ill. His last completed composition is " Eine kleine freymaurer-kantate" (K 623, "A Little Free-Mason Cantata"), which he directed on November 18 in the lodge "To Newly-Crowned Hope" ("Zur neugekrönten Hoffnung"). Two days later he took to his bed; his condition deteriorated rapidly. On December 5, at five minutes before one o'clock in the morning, Mozart died in the presence of his wife, his sister-in-law Sophie and his doctor, Closset.

Much speculation has been raised about the cause of his death, officially recorded as "acute military fever" ("hitziges Frieselfieber"). There were probably several factors working together: a constitution generally weakened by overwork, a rheumatic inflammation perhaps set off by the demonstrably bad weather, and finally the blood-letting prescribed by contemporary medical custom. For the widely circulated myth that he was poisoned—one of the undying legends surrounding Mozart—the few known facts about his death offer no corroboration. Equally untenable is the assertion that he was hurriedly buried in a pauper's grave. In fact, his corpse was laid to rest in the cemetery of St. Marx in conformity to the burial regulations of the time, which forbade pomp. Because the cemetery lay several kilometers from the city, it was not customary for the mourners to follow the coffin to the graveyard, especially since regulations forbade the transport of coffins to the graveyard before six o'clock in the evening, i. e., after dark had broken. The grave site itself was unmarked; burial regulations also forbade placing a cross on the grave. Before the burial a funeral was held in St. Stephan's Cathedral, and in Prague, a memorial mass with 4,000 visitors was read a week later.

son cheval de course. Il raconte à sa femme d'un ton enjoué que, peu après qu'elle soit partie le 7 octobre 1791, il a vendu son «canasson pour 14 ducats»; il a encore fait auparavant deux parties de billard, après quoi il s'est fait apporter du café, a fumé «une excellente pipe» et orchestré «la quasi totalité du rondo du Stadtler», le mouvement final du concerto pour clarinette K. 622. Voici là un compte-rendu dans lequel on ne saurait détecter le moindre indice d'une baisse d'énergie vitale ou créatrice.

En novembre, alors qu'il en est à la moitié du requiem, Mozart tombe malade. Sa dernière composition achevée est «Une petite cantate maçonnique» (K. 623), qu'il dirige le 18 novembre dans la loge «Zur neugekrönten Hoffnung» (A l'espérance nouvellement couronnée). Deux jours plus tard il est alité, et son état s'aggrave rapidement. Le 5 décembre, à une heure moins cinq du matin, il rend l'âme en présence de sa femme, de sa belle-sœur Sophie et de son médecin, le docteur Closset.

On a beaucoup glosé sur la cause de sa mort («violente fièvre militaire»). Elle est vraisemblablement due à un amalgame de plusieurs facteurs, à savoir un affaiblissement de l'état général lié au surmenage, une inflammation rhumatismale peut-être provoquée par le mauvais temps, sans oublier les saignées qui, dans l'état de connaissances qui était celui de l'art médical de l'époque, étaient pratique courante. Quant à la fable largement répandue d'un empoisonnement, les quelques informations dignes de foi quant à la maladie qui aurait entraîné sa mort ne lui reconnaissent aucun fondement. Tout aussi insoutenable est la thèse selon laquelle Mozart aurait été jeté dans une fosse commune. Il est vrai que son corps est inhumé au cimetière Saint-Marx sans la moindre pompe, conformément à la réglementation alors en vigueur en matière d'enterrements. Dans la mesure où le cimetière est situé à quelques kilomètres de la ville, il n'est pas d'usage que le cortège funèbre suive le cercueil jusque là, d'autant que son transfert ne peut avoir lieu, toujours selon la réglementation, qu'à partir de six heures du soir, et donc à la tombée du jour. La tombe reste anonyme. Le protocole funéraire ne permet pas de poser de croix. Des funérailles ont eu lieu auparavant à la cathédrale Saint-Etienne. A Prague est célébrée dès la semaine suivante une messe commémorative à laquelle assistent 4000 personnes.

La veuve de Mozart demande à Franz Xaver Süßmayr de terminer le requiem, le commanditaire ayant

Österreichische 40-Schilling-Briefmarke nach dem Mozart-Porträt von Joseph Lange

Austrian 40-schilling stamp with a picture of Mozart, from the portrait by Joseph Lange

Timbre autrichien de 40 schillings d'après le portrait de Mozart par Joseph Lange

Der Wiener Stephansdom
Kolorierte Radierung nach einem
Aquarell von Carl Schütz, um 1800

St. Stephan's Cathedral in Vienna
Colored etching, from a watercolor by
Carl Schütz, c. 1800

La cathédrale Saint-Etienne à Vienne
Gravure coloriée d'après une aquarelle
de Carl Schütz, vers 1800

setzung mit Graf Walsegg-Stuppach, der Eigentums-
rechte an der Partitur geltend macht.

Nach Mozarts Tod sieht sich Konstanze, die mit
zwei kleinen Kindern dasteht, einem Schuldenberg von
mehr als 1000 Gulden gegenüber. Doch dank der Einnahmen aus Konzerten, die zu ihren Gunsten veran-
staltet werden, gelingt es ihr, die Last zu tilgen. Hinzu
kommen nicht unbedeutende Spenden, Verlagseinnah-
men und Erlöse aus dem Verkauf von Werken aus dem
Nachlaß. Acht davon erwirbt der König von Preußen zu
einem Preis von 3600 Gulden. Auch der Wiener Hof läßt
sie nicht im Stich und gewährt ihr eine kleine Pension.

Im Jahr 1809 heiratet Konstanze Mozart den däni-
schen Diplomaten Georg Nikolaus Nissen, der mit ihr
gemeinsam den Nachlaß verwaltet. Auf seinen Vorar-
beiten beruht die von ihr im Jahr 1828 veröffentlichte
Mozart-Biographie, die das Bemühen verrät, ein ‚gerei-
nigtes‘ Mozart-Bild zu hinterlassen. Dabei gingen beide
so weit, daß sie zahlreiche Briefpassagen unleserlich
gemacht und manche Dokumente – wie die Briefe Kon-
stanzes an ihren Mann – wohl auch unterdrückt haben.
Dennoch ist Nissens Buch verläßlicher als das Gros
jener seit Ende des 18. Jahrhunderts anschwellenden
Mozart-Literatur, in der romanhaft ausgeschmückte
Anekdoten zunehmend die Tatsachen verdrängen. Erst
die vierbändige, wissenschaftlichen Grundsätzen fol-
gende Biographie von Otto Jahn beginnt sich wieder
vom Klischee des verkannten Genies, das in bitterer
Armut starb, zu lösen.

Trotzdem hat sich das romantische, gleichsam
durch die Franz-Schubert-Brille wahrgenommene
Mozart-Bild dem Bewußtsein der Nachwelt bis heute
eingeprägt. Es ist falsch, nicht weil es Mozart vergöttert,
sondern weil es ihn verniedlicht, sein zum ausschwei-
fenden Lebensgenuß neigendes Temperament ins
Biedermännische, seinen derben, oft auch zynischen
Humor ins Naive oder Melancholische verkehrt und aus
dieser Sicht auch seine Werke deutet. Aus Mozarts
Musik spricht eine andere Wahrheit.

Mozart's widow asked Franz Xaver Süssmayr to complete the "Requiem," for the patron had already paid an advance. Süssmayr composed music for the missing elements (Sanctus, Benedictus, Agnus Dei), expanded and orchestrated what he found in Mozart's sketches, and turned to material from the completed "Introit" and "Kyrie" for the "Communion." When Constanze Mozart attempted to have the "Requiem" printed later, she faced opposition from Graf Walsegg-Stuppach, who was able to establish his right of ownership to the score.

The death of her husband left Constanze with two small children and debts amounting to more than 1000 gulden, a sum she was able to repay thanks to the income from concerts that were organized for her benefit. In addition, she was beneficiary of significant donations, income from the publishers, and profit from the sale of works from Mozart's estate. The king of Prussia purchased eight works for a sum of 3,600 gulden. Nor was Mozart's family forgotten by the Viennese court, which granted Constanze a small pension.

In 1809 Constanze Mozart married the Danish diplomat Georg Nikolaus Nissen, who administered the estate jointly with her. Nissen furthermore provided the groundwork for her biography of Mozart, published in 1828, with the clear intention of leaving behind a "purified" image of the composer. The pair went so far as to render numerous passages in the composer's letters illegible, and probably suppressed a number of documents, such as Constanze's letters to her husband. And yet Nissen's biography remains more reliable than most of the growing wave of writings about Mozart that began appearing at the end of the 18th century, in which romantically decorated anecdotes increasingly replaced the truth. The scholarly four-volume biography by Otto Jahn was the first to begin to extricate Mozart from the cliché of the misunderstood genius who died in bitter poverty. Nonetheless, the romantic image of Mozart, perceived through the lens of the life of Franz Schubert, continues to stamp the consciousness of posterity. This view is false not because it deifies Mozart, but because it simplifies and softens him, twists his temperamental proclivity for extravagant indulgence into a Victorian corset, his earthy, often cynical, humor into something naive or melancholic—and then attempts to interpret his works from this perspective. But Mozart's music yields another truth.

versé un acompte. Süßmayr compose les parties manquantes (Sanctus, Benedictus, Agnus Dei), complète et orchestre les ébauches qu'il peut trouver et se sert pour la communion (Lux aeterna) du matériel de l'Introitus et du Kyrie, que Mozart avait achevés. Lorsque Constance Mozart voudra par la suite faire imprimer l'œuvre, elle entrera en conflit avec le comte de Walsegg-Stuppach qui fera valoir ses droits sur la partition.

A la mort de Mozart, Constance se retrouve avec deux jeunes enfants devant une montagne de dettes de plus de 1000 florins. Mais grâce aux recettes provenant de concerts spécialement organisés en sa faveur, elle parvient à l'éponger. A cela s'ajoutent des dons non négligeables, des droits d'auteur ainsi que les produits de la vente d'œuvres posthumes. Le roi de Prusse en acquiert huit pour le prix de 3600 florins. La cour de Vienne ne l'abandonne pas non plus et lui verse une petite pension.

En 1809, Constance Mozart épouse le diplomate danois Georg Nikolaus Nissen, qui gère la succession avec elle. C'est sur les travaux préliminaires de ce dernier que se fonde la biographie publiée par Constance en 1828, et dans laquelle on sent la volonté de donner une image « épurée » de Mozart. Ils sont même allés pour cela jusqu'à rendre illisibles de nombreux passages de la correspondance et à mettre de côté un certain nombre de documents. L'ouvrage de Nissen est néanmoins plus fiable que le gros de toute cette littérature redondante qui sévit à partir de la fin du 18ᵉ siècle et dans laquelle les faits ont de plus en plus tendance à disparaître au profit d'anecdotes et de fioritures romanesques.

Ce n'est qu'avec les quatre volumes de la biographie d'Otto Jahn, qui repose sur des bases scientifiques, que l'on recommence à se détacher du cliché du génie méconnu mort dans le dénuement le plus total.

Et pourtant c'est cette image romantique de Mozart, qui correspond pour ainsi dire à la vision qu'on en aurait en chaussant les lunettes d'un Franz Schubert, qui s'est gravée jusqu'à nos jours dans la conscience de la postérité. Cette image est fausse non parce qu'elle fait de Mozart l'égal d'un dieu, mais parce qu'elle est réductrice. En ramenant en effet son appétit de vivre et son tempérament porté aux débordements à quelque chose de petit-bourgeois, son humour cru et même souvent cynique à de la naïveté ou de la mélancolie, cette vision des choses contamine également l'œuvre. C'est une autre vérité qu'énonce la musique de Mozart.

Erinnerungsmal für Mozart auf dem St. Marxer Friedhof in Wien. Das um 1900 aus Teilen anderer Grabmäler zusammengefügte Monument geht auf die Initiative eines Friedhofswärters zurück. Das 1859 an gleicher Stelle errichtete Mozart-Denkmal von Hans Gasser steht seit 1891 auf dem Wiener Zentralfriedhof.

Memorial to Mozart in the St. Marx Cemetery in Vienna. The monument, constructed around 1900 from parts of other tombstones, derived from the initiative of one of the sextons of the cemetery. The Mozart monument by Hans Glasser that had been erected in 1859 on the same site was removed to the main cemetery in 1891.

Monument à la mémoire de Mozart au cimetière Saint-Marx de Vienne. Ce monument créé en 1900 avec des fragments d'autres tombes est dû à l'initiative d'un gardien de cimetière. Le monument dédié à Mozart de Hans Gasser, édifié en 1859 au même endroit, se trouve depuis 1891 dans le cimetière central.

Credits

Archiv für Kunst und Geschichte, Berlin: Cover, Back cover,
Front flaps, Back flap, and pp. 2, 7–15, 17 right, 18–33, 35–39,
42, 44/45, 47, 48, 50, 51, 53, 54/55, 56, 58, 59, 61–65, 68, 69,
72, 73, 75, 86–89, 91, 92, 95

Columbia, Frankfurt-on-Main: p. 71

Cinetext, Frankfurt: pp. 70, 77–79

East West Records, Hamburg: p. 82

Österreichische Nationalbibliothek, Vienna: Inner back flap
and pp. 80/81

Theaterwissenschaftliche Sammlung der Universität zu Köln,
Schloss Wahn, Cologne: pp. 40/41, 49, 83, 84/85

Any illustrations not listed here come from the author's or
publisher's archive.